# A GUINEA A BOX

# A GUINEA A BOX

## A Biography

# ANNE FRANCIS

Illustrated

HALE · LONDON

© Anne Francis 1968
First published in Great Britain 1968

SBN 7091 0233 X

Robert Hale Limited
63 Old Brompton Road
London S.W.7

PRINTED IN GREAT BRITAIN BY
CLARKE, DOBLE AND BRENDON LTD.,
CATTEDOWN, PLYMOUTH

# CONTENTS

# CONTENTS

# ILLUSTRATIONS

For

# CHRISTOPHER and JUSTIN

# PREFACE

THIS is the story of my great-grandfather, Thomas Beecham. He was the founder of the pill firm which bore his name, already international before his grandson, the conductor, made it a household one twice over. After Thomas Beecham's retirement in 1895 the business continued to be run by his son (Sir) Joseph Beecham. On the latter's death in 1916 it was carried on by Sir Joseph's executors, notably his own son, Henry Beecham, and Charles Rowed, the office manager.

In 1924 the St. Helens business became a public company, Beecham Estates and Pills Ltd. Manufacture was almost entirely confined to Beecham's Pills, with a small turnover in the Cough Pills, discontinued in 1950, whilst Beecham's Powders had been introduced to the home market in 1926.

At the beginning of 1928 a public company, Beecham Pills Ltd., was formed under the chairmanship of Mr. Philip Hill to acquire the medicinal business from Beecham Estates and Pills Ltd. A holding was also secured in the equity of Veno Drug Company, and a prospectus issued stated that further business of this nature would be obtained as opportunities presented themselves. Thereinafter St. Helens saw a fairly steady arrival of new products as this policy was implemented. The metamorphosis was astonishing, and from it has emerged a veritable empire.

Today, Beecham Proprietary Medicines Ltd., is only one unit within the Beecham Group of companies, whilst this, with its many absorptions and mergers, bears very little relationship to the family concern built up by Thomas Beecham and his son, Joseph, and which this book is about. The composition of Thomas's costive pill has been perceptibly altered, and even the factory erected so proudly in the mid 'eighties, has been changed, thousands of square feet, together with a fourth floor, having been added. Yet it must be true to say that without Thomas Beecham's initial efforts the company, in its present form, would be non-existent. Certainly it would flourish under a different name.

For my sources I have drawn on conversations with members of the family, with people who knew Thomas Beecham personally, and some who once worked at the old firm. What material is existent at Beecham Proprietary Medicines, St. Helens, was kindly put my way, and use has been made of books and newspapers of the period.

The list of all those others who have so generously aided me in my research is formidable, and too long to give in detail. But in particular I should like to thank Miss Ruth Bond for her delightful photograph of Thomas Beecham's mother, and Mrs. Matthews for that of him, and his third wife, on horseback. The late Mr. P. R. Templer, gave me information about the Templer family. Both Mrs. Sollis, and Mr. Rowland Beckinsale, for their help in supplying me with details regarding the former Curbridge cottage, and Miss Phyllis Ransom for additional data on Witney. The church archives at Witney and Kidlington yielded rich results, and I am grateful for access to them, whilst in the latter village Mrs. Kemeny, Mr. Salter, Mr. Rowles, and Mr. S. G. Baker were all most patient with my enquiries. I am indebted to Mr. J. F. A. Mason, Christchurch, for facts relating to the Chamberlin family; to Lord Wise for information about the Lawn Farm, Cropredy, and to Mr. Webber for showing me round it. Exhaustive searches were made on my behalf in Liverpool by Mr. S. A. Harris, and in Wigan by Mr. Allan Royle, Town Clerk, and Mr. H. H. G. Arthur, Borough Librarian, and Mr. Mather. My thanks go to Mr. Valentine for information regarding No. 8 New Square, and to Mr. Cowen, Parish Clerk, for dipping into baptismal records for me. In St. Helens Mr. H. C. Caistor, Chief Librarian, Central Library, Mr. Webster, Miss Elsie Morgan, and Mr. Leathwood have all contributed valuable aid. The *Advertiser* files were also put at my disposal. Mrs. Alice Jacobs regaled me with details about the Giles family, and I am extremely sorry that she, and Mrs. Holland, who was so helpful concerning Thomas Beecham's Southport years, have not lived to see the finished book. Mrs. Brooks was hospitable in letting me see his house there. Back numbers of the *Chemist and Druggist* were made available to me by Mr. Shepherd. A *Merseyside Town in the Industrial Revolution St. Helens 1750-1900* by Dr. T. C. Barker and Dr. J. R. Harris has been indispensable, and I have drawn heavily from its pages, as from those of E. S. Turner's *A Shocking History of Advertising*. Last, but far from least, I must acknowledge the encouragement, and very practical assistance rendered by my cousin, Audrey Beecham.

London.                                              A.F.

# PART ONE

# THE SOUTH

# THE LEGEND

THOMAS always liked to keep himself to himself, a trait which deepened as he grew older. Believing, *au fond*, that a man's private affairs are his castle, he seldom lowered the drawbridge to reporters. When he did so, it was only for an instant, exposing the broad outlines but rarely the details of a colourful career. Because of this reticence biographies which appeared in newspapers from time to time after he became well known tended to be apocryphal. Occasionally, and not unnaturally, they contained mistakes, but although indirectly responsible for these, innaccuracies irked their subject, who would promptly seize his pen and dash off a denial to the paper concerned. The procedure tended to be monotonously unvarying; the error would be pointed out, amended, and the matter closed. No elaborations, no lengthy statements, seldom even any penny-plain revelations. Thomas was not to be drawn. Perhaps his longest autobiographical note was that dispatched in old age to a popular magazine.

On 17th May, 1890, readers of this paper learnt, through an innocuous gossip column, that Mlle. de la Ramee, or Ouida, as the world knew her, had given evidence of her literary tastes at the age of four, when she had written a children's story. She lived near Florence, writing outdoors in the summer months in an atmosphere suitably drenched with the scent of orange groves and magnolias. Mrs. Harriet Beecher Stowe was seventy-six. Sir Arthur Sullivan's first musical composition had been an anthem. The Prince of Wales and his son played the banjo, and Mr. Thomas Beecham was originally a shepherd, and lived in the village of Granborough, in Buckinghamshire. Lately he had purchased an estate and erected a mansion within a few miles of his birth-place, and spent upwards of £30,000 a year in advertising.

If they read this chit-chat the other celebrities were content to let the information, true or untrue, rest. Not so Thomas, who was soon splitting hairs. "I was sitting in my office yesterday," he enlightened the editor of *Tit-Bits*, the magazine in question, "when I came across a part respecting myself which somewhat amused me, and as my name is pretty well known and your paper has a wide circulation, I have no doubt the said paragraph will be read by some hundreds with no small amusement to each. . . !"

Pretty well known? A gross under-statement to say the least, and one which possibly provoked an editorial smile or two on its own account! For by this date Thomas was the largest advertiser in the United Kingdom. Also, and as he was careful to stipulate, more than three times the sum quoted had been spent on advertising the previous year—£95,000 in fact, a staggering sum for those days. Pills rolled out of the cutting machine at the rate of 15,000 a minute, or 9,000,000 in a normal working day of ten hours. Sufficient, an enterprising statistician had reckoned, to give the whole population of Ireland or London a mild aperient every night. By the end of this year no less than six million boxes would have been sold, while an annual £90,000 was being spent on patent medicine stamps. Fame was indeed now so assured that a traveller in Africa said to have congratulated himself he was blazoning a remote trail where no other white foot had trodden, was chagrined to find, painted on a tree in native language, an advertisement for Beecham's Pills.

But Thomas's pen, scratching on, eschewed jokes. Himself and his products he took in deadly earnest. He had never, he declared, mis-spelling it, lived in Grandborough, and knew nothing at all about it. Nor had he ever bought ". . . an estate and built a mansion thereon within a few miles of my birth-place. Your informant tells you Thomas Beecham was originally a shepherd, which is truth. . . . Very early in my teens I took charge of the entire flock, and stuck to it till I was twenty years of age. A slight turn in the tide of events caused me to give it up. I may here say that for some years before the above age a thirst for a little knowledge of humanity had sprung up within me; a slight wave of opportunity presented itself; and I launched my tiny barque on the ever-shifting sea of commercial uncertainty. I have no cause to complain," he continued grandiloquently, "for, after fifty years of hard work and practical experience, I can now look back and take a survey of the keen, competing crowd who are struggling daily on the ocean of life, and say to myself, 'I envy none of you'." In conclusion he had "seen seventy Christmas Days, and am thankful to tell you I am as bright for work as ever."

The pen stopped. Enough, if not too much, had been disclosed! Fractionally dipped, the drawbridge was hurriedly re-hoisted.

Appearing in the magazine's next issue this letter went un-challenged. The column was composed of readers' contributions, and whoever the correspondent was he, or she, stood corrected.

In professing ignorance of Granborough Thomas had been guilty of planting a red herring in the informant's path. Not only did he have a sister there, but for years she and her family, of whom he saw a good deal, had lived in a neighbouring village. He could *not* have known the place. Again, an estate and moderate-sized mansion certainly existed, if not in his actual birth-place, at any rate relatively near as the crow flew. By evasion of the whole truth, however, he probably hoped to dis-courage further snoopers. And as it happened he was in the process of relinquishing this property which had been a painful episode in his life, and one which doubtless he was only too anxious to gloss over. Mursley Hall had been built approximately eleven years before when doctors had advised him to take things more easily. Since then much had occurred to lure him back to the north. Health was improved. His third wife had left him, and a pill palace had replaced his old, plain factory. Business was expanding at an enormous rate, exciting new markets were opening up. His son, Joseph, who ran the firm in his absence, was now a prominent citizen in the town. The Beechams, who only a short while back, had been virtual nonentities, were news.

Metronomically dividing his time between the south and the north Thomas, when in St. Helens, slept at the firm. His day began precisely as it ended. A stroll through the various depart-ments, a thundered greeting to employees encountered en route, but no small talk. He had never been addicted to this, and men who had toiled with him in more mundane surroundings, understood and were not offended. They, and Thomas, belonged to an era visibly crumbling under their noses. One in which they had sweated twelve hours a day to the boss's fourteen or sixteen. When there had been no cosseting, few if any half holidays, recreation grounds or annual excursions. When, if there *had* have been time for such niceties, the business, of which they were almost as proud as its founder, could not possibly have scaled its present pinnacle.

To adolescents, who often totalled a third of the staff, Thomas was an awesome legend. Semi-retired, despite his boast he was as bright as ever for work, he acted more in an advisory capacity than anything else, and it was the quietly spoken Mr. Joseph Beecham who was the presiding genius. But if they had the slightest pretension to wits, they respected the legend when it bore down upon them across the picking or filling room floors. Were careful to be on time, not to be caught whispering or idling, to be clean and tidy. Punctuality, industry, cleanliness, these were not so much Beecham standards as Beecham commandments. And Thomas it was who had first hacked out the statutes.

Ironically enough if Thomas ever did stop to talk to anyone, it was to the boys he did not know, rather than to the men he did. Though he might not be much in evidence now, he still took great interest in the employees, and was quick to spot a new face. Below his brusque manner he could be surprisingly sympathetic. His had been a gruelling apprenticeship, and consequently he liked to put youngsters at ease. In doing so he was magnificently unaware that his patriarchal exterior, bushy beard, and piercing gaze inspired panic, rather than confidence. "Conversations" were apt to be as brief as press interviews, and as flatly unprogressive. How long (a gruff bark) had the boy been at Beecham's? A fortnight. And he was how old? Thirteen, sir. His first job? Yes. H'm! An imperiously Beecham snap and crackle of the blue eyes, a shouted good-bye, and Thomas, moving at a licking pace, was already half way out of the department before relieved youth could wonder if it had given the wrong answer. It was not to know that by the same age Thomas had been at work five, health-sapping years.

Joseph now lived at Huyton, a small village some six miles distant, and half way on the road to Liverpool. If he was in England Thomas sometimes stayed with him. Joseph's coachman, Tom Oldham, would drive both men over in the firm's brougham. Oldham, who had worked with Thomas as a boy, wore a smart navy livery with a striped zebra waistcoat. Carriage people were then the élite of society, and tremendous competition raged between the grooms to have the best turn-out. In this Oldham more than held his own. His uniform would have satisfied the most exacting sergeant-major, while carriage and horses were rubbed till they gleamed like satin. In striking contrast to so much spit and polish were the occupants of the vehicle. A contemporary has described Joseph as being so unassuming he could have been taken for his own butler, and on at least one occasion he was. Certainly his unpretentious clothes did not suggest a pill fortune, whilst Thomas's ancient frock coat, paper collar, and the hard round hat he wore in and out of season were even less congruous.

The way to Huyton never altered. The brougham clattered along Westfield Street, onto which the main entrance of the factory opened. At the fork further along, Cropper's Hill with its steep incline which was considered injurious to the horses, was avoided, and instead Oldham steered them up the gentler slope of Borough Road. The top gained the air blew refreshingly brighter, and below the town sprawled in an ugly rash of red buildings, Beecham's, with its splendid clock tower, the one aesthetic touch. As the horses spanked along Prescot Road the clear, musical chimes echoed behind them and vied with their hooves. Still fairly rural in these parts, industrialism gradually slipped away, cottages, farms, and orchards appearing with pleasing frequency.

Arrived at Ewanville, Joseph's home, Thomas would occupy himself during the interval before dinner poking and prying into rooms, cupboards, and even bins, with the endless curiosity he displayed in everything. A tour of inspection might include a visit to the nursery where, in a wing especially built for them, the younger grandchildren were cared for by two nurses. These excursions were usually conducted, and endured, in complete silence. For the virtual toddler Thomas had nothing to say, whilst the normally vociferous little Beechams were struck dumb by their grandfather's antediluvian appearance. So much hair, such a sense of sheer physical *power*, made Thomas appear larger than he was, also faintly alarming.

Depending upon the temperament of the diner a meal at Ewanville could be an event, or a crashing bore. Thomas endorsed the latter viewpoint. As he had written he had once been a shepherd. Shepherd ways persisting with him he preferred to eat as appetite, and not the clock, dictated, paying minimum attention to manners, and maximum to stuffing his mouth. Joseph, who had not been a shepherd, who had, moreover, a fastidious wife, sometimes served up as many as seven courses on a table always beautifully appointed. Soft-footed servants swooping around reverently laid down plates, snatched up others. Breathing down his neck they did not inhibit Thomas, who could never personally have known the meaning of the word. They merely bogged down a function which was as natural as walking, and which would have taken a quarter of the time it did without so much unnecessary paraphernalia.

A welcome divertissement in the cloying gradeur, and joining the adults at dessert, might be Joseph's two eldest children, Emily and Tom, aged respectively sixteen and eleven. Joseph's household was typically Victorian in that children were expected to be seen and not heard, to reply only when spoken to. Since, the antithesis of Thomas, Joseph tended to be non-loquacious. this

B

seldom happened. But with his father such tacit rules went by
the board. Thomas had not been reared in luxury, but in a three-
roomed cottage cluttered with sisters and brothers all fighting,
arguing, and tripping over each other for *lebensraum*. So long
as his voice was raised the loudest, heard the most, and went
uncontradicted, anyone here, and in contrast to the monastic
quiet at the factory, was at liberty to speak. In common, also,
with many parents at variance with their own offspring, Thomas
was capable of outrageously spoiling other people's.

Dinner over at last, and if he was in a mellow mood, Thomas
might command his grandson and namesake to thump out a
tune on the piano. Either the grand one which stood in the
sumptuous drawing-room, or the upright piano placed in a
passage-way leading to the conservatories. The fact that Thomas
was utterly unmusical did not deter him from listening to young
Tom with benign enjoyment. The faster and more furious the
pace the better he liked it. Such facility proved that the boy
was not wasting time at his lessons. To slack, to throw good
money after bad, these were venial sins in Thomas's private
catechism.

What remained of the evening could be passed in one of half-
a-dozen ways, all equally interesting. Discussing business affairs
with Joseph . . . orders, exports . . . the American market . . .
being brought up to date with the advertising, the medium
which had changed so startlingly since Thomas had first ventured
into it nearly three decades ago. Or, if Joseph preferred to drift
off to the billiards room and engross himself at the organ there,
Thomas was content to sink back in his chair, settle his reading
glasses, and browse through chemical manuals. Possibly because
he was always occupied he had the supreme gift of never being
bored. Ewanville was wonderfully peaceful, wonderfully relaxing. . . .

Outside, well-stocked hot-houses flanked the building, and
beyond the bay windows immaculately kept lawns shelved away
to a rich man's paddocks. As yet the view from the front was
unurbanised, miles of meadows pressing up moistly against the
horizon, beyond which were other villages, more fields, and the
River Mersey. The pastoral world of Thomas's own childhood,
yet with a subtle difference. Affluence abounded.

Thomas was essentially a person who lived in the present. He
did not grumble because rising generations were luckier than he
had been. In fact, he went a great way towards ensuring they
*were*. And though he sometimes alluded to, he never complained
about, early hardship. "That there is no such thing as complete

happiness upon earth is a very old truism." He had marked this observation where it had occurred in a pamphlet on palmistry he carried around with him. Yet if ever a human being was whole-heartedly happy it was himself. Early environment had first hampered, then egged him on. In hauling himself from the rut of poverty it had been vital to be single-minded about his pill. But he had many gifts, and without the need to dedicate himself so totally to the job on hand might have succeeded just as spectacularly in several walks of life. As a writer, an orator, a doctor, or even in a different business. Fantastically, however, and given the chance all over again had it been possible, the odds are that he would have wished nothing changed. He had no social aspirations, no envy, no wish to step into anyone else's shoes.

It was partly the reluctance to dwell in the past which made him impatient about discussing it with reporters. But sometimes if they, or an incident, jogged his memory, he permitted himself a fleeting glance over his shoulder. A look invariably accompanied by a complacent pat of self-approval. Pills being turned out at the rate of 15,000 a minute; tenpence of every shilling profit ploughed back into advertising; property, servants, carriages—particularly carriages—it was all vastly satisfactory. A far cry, indeed, across seventy crowded Christmases to the tiny Oxfordshire village where the story first began.

2

# A VILLAGE BOYHOOD

A T the edge of the Cotswolds, some twelve miles from Oxford and two out of the ancient town of Witney, famed for its breweries and blanket mills, lies the hamlet of Curbridge. Off the beaten track it is quite unremarkable. Many of the older dwellings are fashioned of grey stone, whose slate roofs give the place a singularly drab aspect. Together with the modern bungalows and telegraph poles they peter away into the flat countryside, where the only building of any interest is a moated mansion dating back to Tudor times.

Today Curbridge's population is well under five hundred. At the turn of the nineteenth century it was even smaller. Little more than a scatter of barns and cottages dotted about between the lanes, and under the high elms. Although wool had started to be imported from the colonies, sheep grazed there in fair numbers, and the more important farms had not been broken up. Except for the two inns, the Herd and Swine (now the Lord Kitchener), and the Merry Horn, a beer-cum-slaughter-house on the way to the downs which today form part of Witney Aerodrome, there were few amenities, no school or church. Consequently the fruits of boredom, petty cases of felony, assault, and bastardy, swelled the assize records. Isolated incidents of wifeselling, usually for a few shillings, also occurred. Village life itself was simple, uncomplicated, and existed on three levels— the gentry, the respectable folk, who included anyone above the position of labourer, and the poor people. Between the first two groups, and the last, there was no fraternising, not even in church, where the labourer filed in after everyone else and sat in a separate pew.

The Beechams belonged categorically to the poor people. Their origin in this Oxfordshire backwater is obscure, though it is thought that one or more of their ancestors may have landed with William the Conqueror from Normandy, in time the French Beauchamp becoming anglicised. Tradition also has it that late in the seventeenth century they were property owners in a small way. For some reason, however, they plunged downhill, and never regained status. What is certain in a welter of conjecture, is that they were always connected with the land in some form or other. As a clan they tended to be industrious, painstaking, and persevering. Proud in their penury they kept clear of the hated overseer, troubled few Justices of the Peace, and had a near genius for anonymity.

In 1792 James Beecham, a farm worker, and the first who can be traced in an unbroken line through the local archives, married a Charlotte Lowry whose lineage is unknown, since she came from a different parish. The couple had three children; Mary born in 1793, William 1796, and Joseph three years later. Eventually William settled in another village where he married and became a shepherd. Slightly more will be heard of him later. In 1819 Mary married a local labourer, Jesse Templer. A martinet, she was fiercely ambitious for her children. One daughter was to become a school teacher, an unusual occupation for a girl at that period in that class. A son, Thomas, born about a year after her wedding, she sent to school, again a far from customary practice for her kind. The boy proved a natural scholar, and Mary encouraged him to study in his attic room, often late at night by the glow of a tallow candle. This, though his father, who could see no sense in a child of his being educated, beat him for his pains. Also extremely musical, Thomas Templer later emigrated to South Africa, where he made good, and composed pieces for wind instruments, and set psalms to music.

Like his father, Joseph was a labourer, then a shepherd. Throughout the year his sister was adjusting herself to her new life he was busy courting a fair-haired, animated girl, slightly younger than himself, whose parents lived in the village, and whose father, James Hunt, was a farm worker. When finally Joseph married Sarah Hunt on 4th October, 1820, at Witney Parish Church, she was seven months pregnant. As his sister had done before him, Joseph signed the register, which meant he could at least write his name. But Sarah, being wholly illiterate, contented herself with making a cross.

No reason has ever come down for Joseph's delay in honouring his bride. Though it was common enough in rural areas for a prospective groom to ensure his future wife's fertility by "anticipating the honeymoon", in leaving matters so late Joseph certainly erred on the side of caution! Parental objection may have been another impediment, for unlike the Beechams the Hunts had a wild streak in their nature. Hot-blooded, perpetually in and out of trouble, they were particularly feckless with money, which they squandered on drink. Older sisters, too, can be domineering, and Mary, with ideas well above her station, may have hoped Joseph would have made a better match. However, he might simply have experienced difficulty in finding a home. Cottages were apt to go with the jobs, farmers being employers and landlords combined.

The boy born to the couple at exactly 11.34 p.m. on 3rd December, was christened Thomas Beecham a fortnight later at the Parish Church. His youthful parents settled down in a grey stone cottage just off the Witney to Bampton road, and round the corner from today's council house estate. This building had two bedrooms and a single room downstairs, where meals were cooked on an open stove. No windows faced the front, but at the rear overlooked a field rich with herbs, belonging to the owners of Caswell Farm, the moated mansion already mentioned, and visible in the middle distance. A low wall divided it from the next-door cottage, and the small garden contained a well, and an enormous holly bush. Though ownership has been impossible

to establish, it was assuredly not freehold, and may well have
been the property of Dutton's Farm opposite, where Joseph is
said to have worked. Pulled down some time during the First
World War, the present "Beecham Cottage" erected approximately over the former site, though not large, is considerably
more spacious. By this date George IV sat on the throne. Lord
Liverpool was Prime Minister; Charles Dickens was eight years
old; the battle of Waterloo had raged five years earlier, and the
Agrarian and Industrial Revolutions were well under way.

Very little is known of Thomas's father. Joseph had, or
developed, a melancholy disposition, whilst, as the years passed,
the responsibility of rearing a growing family on an inadequate
wage seriously undermined a constitution far from strong.

Times for the agricultural labourer, who was enduring the
aftermath of the French Revolutionary and Napoleonic Wars,
were exceptionally hard. While these had been in progress the
farmers had grown corn in vast quantities, but afterwards, when
the price slumped, a law was passed prohibiting the import of
corn until the price on the home market reached 80s. a quarter.
A short-sighted policy, since, by making bread dearer the poor
people were unable to buy such staple products as eggs, butter,
cheese, and meat. Earlier, in 1795 when rioting had broken out
in the southern counties, magistrates meeting in Speenhamland,
Berkshire, had devised a system, still in operation. By it the
labourer received a certain weekly sum from the parish, which
fluctuated with the price of bread, and was in addition to his
wage. But like the corn law it was a two-edged remedy, because
the labourer was reduced to the level of a pauper dependent on
parish money, though saved from actual starvation. Employers
began to pay the lowest possible wage, and the poor law soared
to absurd figures.

Other injustices abounded. Acts of enclosure going on all over
the country robbed the labourer of grazing land and firewood.
At this period the real governors of the country were the J.P.s
and the squires. Terrified of a spread of French Jacobinism
amongst the working classes, they suppressed them by cruel laws.
House-breaking and sheep-stealing were checked by capital
punishment; not until 1838 did anyone cease to be hanged for
an offence other than murder. Equally harsh were gaming laws.
A poacher could, if caught at sight with his nets on him, be
transported for seven years. Hidden mantraps and spring guns
protecting pheasant preserves frequently maimed the innocent
as well as the guilty, and were only abolished in 1827.

Happily, the Joseph Beechams were not troubled by much of the above at the outset of their marriage. For a few years acute poverty could be kept at bay. Curbridge was not enclosed until after 1838, while it was possible to grow vegetables in the little garden. And, though burdened with a baby from the beginning, nearly three years elapsed before a second was born. Thus the meagre wages vacillating between nine and twelve shillings a week, sometimes less, could be stretched to include the necessities of life, if not the luxuries. This was just as well, for at first Thomas was so sickly that at one point his life was actually despaired of. "Doctors", he was to recall, "were not much good in those days." Good, bad, or indifferent, they were well beyond the cottager's purse, and Sarah, though young, and in common with her kind, had recourse to salves and simples. Her skill was considerable, for Thomas survived, though poor health was to dog him indefinitely.

Working seven days a week at his job, Joseph's leisure was scant, and the dominant personality in the boy's life was the mother. Except that Sarah was robust, Thomas physically resembled her, being small, blue-eyed, and flaxen-haired. Both had the same narrow hands with extraordinarily long fingers. In later photographs of Thomas it is these fingers which first rivet the attention. They shared identical temperaments, also, being fun-loving, snappy, and charged with immense vitality. Thomas was devoted to Sarah, as was she to him. He was to be endlessly generous to her, and the link forged between them in these formative years remained unbroken until her death.

Childhood was far from lonely. For company, before his four sisters and two brothers arrived, Thomas had his Templer cousin to play with, besides other relations who called in, or were visited, Sarah being sociably inclined.

Dandled on various knees in innumerable cottages, the boy's quick imagination was fed with stories of the supernatural, as well as other kinds. As a family the Beechams were given to clairvoyance. Belief in witchcraft and black magic was so prevalent in the countryside at that time that spells were inextricably woven into parlour games. Several houses in Witney were reputed to be haunted, whilst two old women, not long before, were supposed to have communicated with the Evil One. One had transformed herself into a *hare*. Lolloping about on Curbridge Downs she had been shot in the leg by a farmer, in proof of which she remained permanently lame!

Since antiquity, also, cottage cures had gone hand in hand with superstition. A dish of water placed under the bed effectively removed cramp, while warts could be spirited away. In a sheep-rearing area it was natural that these animals should come to be closely associated with health. Patellas of sheep or lambs were placed by the credulous under pillows to dispel muscular pains. Remedies for respiratory complaints, including consumption, were often attempted by making the invalid walk about amongst a flock, or even by driving a few sheep into the house for several nights, and sleeping near them. Naïve as these cures sound, they were nevertheless imbedded in country logic, wool being thought to absorb infection. Years later, when the Prince of Wales contracted typhoid fever, it was seriously opined that healing could be hastened by wrapping him in a sheepskin still warm from the animal.

The labourer's lot would have proved unbearable had it not been for the light relief he enjoyed in the shape of fairs and circuses. In Witney these were wonderful events! Farm hands paraded to be hired at the annual Mop Fair, the carters standing in one spot with their whips, the shepherds with their crooks in another, and so on. But by far the biggest excitement was Witney Feast Day. Falling in September it lasted four whole days, the green being transformed into a fairyland of swings, stalls, and merry-go-rounds. The whole world seemed to pour into town. Freaks, actors, clowns, quacks, and the vivid here-today-gone-tomorrow men who sold anything from love charms to potions. Their rapid patter, often delivered in a strange dialect, sounded distinctly foreign. Yet even when they could be only partially understood they triumphed by sheer force of argument. Sometimes as much money passed between them and their gullible clients in one hour as Joseph earned in an entire week! The opportunity, of course, for the labourer to capitalize on his own talents was too good to be missed. Extra shillings could be acquired by carving and varnishing walking sticks, sold to visitors. Thomas was to excel at this, Joseph possibly teaching him.

Rounding off this marvellous feast would be a day spent in the nearby Forest of Wychwood, where literally thousands of people assembled at once for a giant picnic. Though they could be appallingly quarrelsome amongst themselves, the Beechams were very gregarious, and aunts, uncles, grandparents and children swarmed with the rest of the townsfolk into the glades. It was very gay, very irresponsible, and in old age Thomas called the last house he built for himself "Wychwood" in memory of these boisterous junketings.

Further enchantment was provided in summer by Morris dancers, and at Christmas by mummers, who inspired Thomas with a life-long love of the theatre. And every week, for a boy with a bright mind and an observant eye, there was the fascination of Thursday market day. Stalls laden with old boots, iron crooks, smocks, gingerbread, and patent medicines, were set out under Witney Buttercross. The square mazed over with hurdles, clatter growing deafening as sheep and pigs were driven in and penned. The thrill of the auctions would be followed by the clearing up and washing down. Suddenly, out of thin air, and before the crowds had dispersed, one of the here-today-gone-tomorrow men would materialize. Quick as lightning he formed a ring round himself, launched into his patter, and interest was whipped up all over again.

Unusually responsive, Thomas liked Witney. The quaint Cotswold stone houses flanking the commons. The shops, the beautiful church with its elegant windows and turret pinnacles; the arched gates of hostelries where, not so far back in time, pack-horses laden with merchandise from Wales and Herefordshire had paused on their way to London. Best of all he enjoyed watching the carriages of the gentry and the respectable folk clip-clopping along the gracious High Street. To ride in his own one day became a deep passion.

In 1823 Sarah gave birth to a daughter, called Leah. Far from having his thunder stolen, Thomas, who had a natural paternal streak, was delighted with the newcomer.

Leah seemed to trigger off more births, for two years later sister Mary was born, and yet another girl, Jane, in 1827. Now the domestic picture was drastically changed. The cottage which had been ample for three, even four, people, with six elbowing and crawling around, shrank to minute proportions. Like Thomas the little girls were highly charged and exuberant. Old enough to play with their brother, Leah and Mary found him a stimulating companion. He had crude good humour, was admirably inventive. But, and as they quickly discovered, this god also possessed feet of clay. He was bossy, obstinate, fiery tempered. Thomas's rages, which were to become a byword, no doubt originated from a sharp intelligence continually being slowed down by lesser ones. For Sarah it was a trying time. What with the additional work, the closeness of the quarters, the constant bickering, her patience—like her son's never her strong point—became sorely tested. Possibly it was in an endeavour to procure a minimum of peace that she packed "Our Tom" off to school some time around his seventh year. It was a bold decision. Places at country schools were seldom more than half filled. Farmers wanted cheap labour, parents needed money, and these two facts served to keep children out of the classrooms. Additionally, education tended to reduce a child's market value. Because of the danger of fermenting unrest farmers were against instruction of the poor. But Sarah may well have had another, even more human reason. Tom Templer was going to school. Perhaps she wanted to prove her own son the equal of her lofty-minded sister-in-law's.

Which of the free establishments in Witney Thomas attended is not known. The National Schools, primarily aimed at the promotion of Christian knowledge, had been set up in the town hall in 1813. There also existed the William Blake school, endowed in the eighteenth century, and if anything more painfully pro-selytizing. Here, children whose parents had to be both poor and indigent (Joseph more than qualified!) were perfected in the catechism, as well as reading. Admitted at six years of age, they were expected to continue to nine, or if leaving before to have read the Bible twice. Long before adolescence was finished Thomas knew his Bible backwards. His ardour was his own, his parents being regular, rather than dedicated churchgoers. Sarah is thought to have hailed from a Methodist background, but if so "chapel" would have been played down, since labourers had been known to lose their jobs and cottages if their persuasion was openly admitted.

If Sarah hoped her Tom would turn into a scholar like his cousin whose nose, once shown one, stayed gued to a desk, she was disappointed. Though Thomas learnt to read quickly, he was no bookworm. In fact, he wasted his time, occasionally playing truant, his nature being too mercurial to relish kicking his heels together for hours in a musty classroom. There may even have been a hint of patronage on teacher's part. Instilling the Three Rs into recalcitrant youngsters who would speedily forget everything in lives sacrificed to manual drudgery must have been soul destroying to the extreme. If so, Thomas, imbued with a full measure of Beecham pride, would have been swift to detect and resent it. "At school," Templer was to recollect, a shade smugly, "we were known as the two Toms. Tom Beecham was not very brilliant, and I had to help him."

School might be irksome, but mercifully it was of short dura-tion.

Joseph's slender means were now strained to their limit. No longer could he afford to have Thomas idle, and accordingly the boy was pulled from his lessons and set to work in the fields. Eight years old "the brief holiday with childhood" was over. Its

influences had been profound. The sturdy, ebullient mother, the
close-knit family circle. Village cures, fairs and markets. The line
of demarcation neatly, but sharply segregating the poor people
from the rest of the world. And last, but far from least, the
carriages that other, so unfairly favoured hemisphere, sat in.

3

## CROPREDY

HIS wages were "1s. 6d. per week of seven days."

If the modern mind recoils from the idea of a delicate child
set to do a man's work long before the age of puberty, it might
be as well to glance briefly at the times again.

Though reformers such as Sir Robert Peel the elder had been
agitating for state control of children in factories, their ill-usage
died hard. The Act of 1802 limiting child labour to twelve hours
a day without night work had applied only to paupers in cotton
mills. And it was at the textile industry that a fresh Act in 1819,
prohibiting employment of anyone under the age of nine was
directed. Fourteen more years were to pass before children below
this age came to be excluded from working in factories; the
hours under thirteen restricted to forty-eight a week, or adolescents under twelve made to attend school for a minimum two
hours a day. While almost another decade would grind by before
women, and children below ten, were forbidden to work in mines,
though small boys would be pushed up chimneys by brutal
masters until 1864, the year after Charles Kingsley had penned
his blistering *Water Babies*.

In such circumstances, therefore, the little Thomas might be
said to have been almost fortunate. Employed outdoors his lungs
were not infected by the moist air of an over-heated factory. Nor
was he flogged to keep awake, obliged to crawl on all fours along
a dark coal shaft. He was not a pauper, bound by the parish,
and dispatched in a waggon without any hope of redress to the
proprietor of a cotton mill.

Yet the next few years seemed interminable, and though they
hurt, speaking of them much later, Thomas was to be typically

succinct. He worked on several farms in the vicinity, "tending sheep in the open field", sometimes sleeping at, sometimes away from, home. One of his jobs entailed minding sheep on Curbridge Downs, where the old woman of the anecdote had romped. If alone there all night even the stoutest heart must have quailed during the long vigils where every sound would be frighteningly magnified! Though treated well enough by some employers, others made him eat his meals with the animals, whilst farmer's wives were not above administering sound beatings. Irrepressible by temperament, Thomas was never more so than in times of trouble. Such buoyancy could all too easily be misconstrued as subversive cockiness by employers hounded by the bogey of French Jacobinism. It went to show what they were so fond of saying, that a little learning was a dangerous thing. Thomas was often hungry, too. So famished, that he was driven to stealing turnips which he devoured raw. Not unnaturally his health remained "like a creaking gate". But with inherited instinct he searched for remedial herbs in the fields. Had a good fairy wished this form of self-help on him over his cradle, she could not have bestowed a greater gift. As a result of such trial and selection Thomas developed a cast iron stomach, so that it was to be said of him that the only poison he could not swallow without injury was prussic acid.

In this bleak desert of time the grey stone cottage with its rough and ready affection was the saving oasis into which he tumbled at night, or returned to whenever possible. To the admiring sisters he was now more of a god than ever, being that most prized being, a bread winner.

A second boy, born to Sarah in 1830, was christened James after his paternal grandfather. The Beechams tended to perpetuate names. The same year saw a dramatic change for the worse in the labourer's lot. Once more violence erupted in the southern counties. Farm workers rioted in support of their demand for a living wage of half-a-crown a day. Ricks were burned, and detested threshing machines, considered to be a source of unemployment, destroyed. These outrages were heralded by anonymous letters dispatched to farmers, and macabrely signed "Swing". To quell the rebels special constables were sworn in, troops summoned. After the disturbances had been resolved the revenge taken by the judges was very terrible. Three rioters were hanged, and more than four hundred others torn from their families and deported to Australia. Though no Beechams, Hunts or Templers were involved, the events had the same sobering effect on them as on the rest of the labouring poor folk. Forbidden to protest or band together, the farm worker no longer had a fighting chance. As far as he could see the horizon was back, and only two choices remained. To knuckle under, or attempt different employment in one of the towns mushrooming up in the textile centres in the north of England, and which provided cheap labour for the new industries.

Ten years were to elapse before Thomas made his own decision. When he did he found a third way out.

In middle age Thomas wrote feelingly of ". . . the miserable condition such as all are placed in who work their lives out on a farm for a few paltry shillings a week." However, he was far too conscientious not to give of his best, even in dead-end work. A perfectionist, with painstaking application to detail in anything he undertook, possessing a flair for veterinary medicine, he was, in fact, peculiarly suited to shepherding. And as he grew older, and was accorded greater responsibility, he derived genuine pleasure from his own skill. Already farmers were finding that the Cotswold sheep which had originally been the basis of prosperity in that region in the fifteenth century, made better mutton than wool. But Thomas would have undoubtedly cared for this breed, the animals with tufts of wool hanging over their foreheads as far as their nostrils. Leicesters, and South Downs with their pretty speckled faces, also grazed in that area. Shepherding was a patchwork business. Incredibly slow-moving in late summer and autumn. Conversely hectic at lambing time, when a shepherd might expect to work not only from dawn to dusk, but half the night as well. Shearing, usually occurring in June, was another busy period. Often hired helps were engaged, bands of men who worked at furious speed, were racy and colourful as gypsies, and brought a welcome breath of the outside world to the farms. The season over, they would fade chameleon wise into more mundane past-times such as hedging or ditching until summer came round again.

The job was not for the squeamish. In those days before spraying was known, doctoring sheep was a messy affair, particularly when ridding them of maggots. They were subject to many illnesses, including giddiness induced by tapeworms, and liver fluke, which, following a wet season, could reduce a flock by half. Primitive, too, was castration—the means by which the male reproductive organs are removed, and a ram lamb turned into a wether one. Frequently is was effected by the teeth. Shepherds' clothes were specialized. Invariably they included a smock made of hemp or flax, and with no opening back or front for wind protection. Cloaks, worn in cold weather, had capacious pockets into one of which a sharp knife would be pushed, and they were often brushed over with a preparation of boiled oil to render them waterproof. Crooks, for picking out and holding down sheep, were made of iron, fashioned by the local blacksmith to the shepherd's own design. Straw hats in summer, felt in winter, laced boots, stout breeches, and enormous gigs, or umbrellas, completed the ensemble. As idiosyncratic as his garments could be the wearer himself. Since most of the decisions arising in his work had to be faced by him alone, he was both intensely individual, and king of the agricultural world. When the welfare of a flock depended almost entirely on the shepherd's skill, the farmer made certain of his employee. Qualities of dependability, responsibility, initiative, were not so much desirable as vital.

Shepherding moulded Thomas's nature, developed his talents, and in a sense never left him. Shepherd ways, traits, and habits persisted throughout his days. Even when he could afford fine clothes, garments were bought primarily for service and lasting value, rather than display. Covering huge distances on foot, he always preferred walking to riding. And he moved, even in advanced age, with the shepherd's upright gait, swinging out freely, an invisible flock behind him. He retained the priceless habit of being able to curl up on the hardest surface at a moment's notice and indulge in forty winks. Dedication to the job had to be total, observation acute. No detail in his own work was ever to escape Thomas, whilst his powers of concentration were prodigious. Despite poor health, long exposure to the elements hardened him, so that he acquired amazing stamina. Solitary so much, he became inventive, a thinker, self-reliant—also arrogant and opinionated. The cream of shepherding lay in the markets. Now the youthful Thomas was a participant in these excitements, instead of a mere onlooker, attending auctions for the selling and replacement of flocks, helping to drive the sheep into the towns, chain the dog, proudly plant his crook in a corner of the pen alongside those of the older men. And, as significantly, picking up their hard, sexy, uninhibited conversation.

It may have been at the Mop Fair, or through the labourer's grapevine, that Thomas heard of a job going with Mr. William Hunt Chamberlin at the Lawn Farm, Cropredy, near Banbury.

Chamberlin, to whom Thomas went in his eleventh or twelfth year, was then a bachelor approaching his mid-fifties, a semi-recluse, and a progressive farmer. Some of his ideas were ahead of his time, as is evidenced by a treaty he had printed in 1818. In it he attacked the poor law system by which labourers' wages were made up out of parish funds. Instead, he devised a plan whereby the farmer paid the workers according to their respective merits, in open competition, personally selecting those he wished to employ. This humane scheme carried the dignity of non-interference with actual wages. Chamberlin had the courage to act on it successfully enough to see it adopted both in Cropredy, and in adjacent villages by other discriminating employers. Various magistrates in Oxfordshire and Northamptonshire also sanctioned it. He came of sound farming stock. His father, John Chamberlin, who farmed The Lawn before him, hailed from Leicestershire, and was a well-known enclosure commissioner whose views on farming had been considered so important by Arthur Young, a former secretary of the Board of Agriculture, that he quoted them five times in his report on the agriculture of Oxon. Both father and son described themselves as land surveyors.

Owners of the Lawn Farm, a grey rangey house, were the Cope family of Hanwell Castle, Oxfordshire, and Bramshill Park, Hampshire. A picture executed in 1842 shows it to be little changed since Thomas's time there, except that no railway bisected the fields, nor was there a long drive leading up to the building from Oxhey Hill at the bottom, as it climbs towards Mollington. A charming dovecote also stood in the garden, and the farm itself was then much closer to the village with its attractive yellow stone cottages. Master and servants slept in the house. The new shepherd's home was a stone cottage at the back of which was a lambing field. One up and one down, deepset windows kept it dim as a church, and it opened out three ways, including directly into the stables. Everywhere the land stretched very exposed, and this preponderancy to draughts made it icy in winter, even when a fire was burned in the downstairs grate, the upper shutters pulled to.

A long way in mileage from Curbridge, the decision to move young, and far from home, which he could neither have had the opportunity or the money to visit often, was a momentous one. But any homesickness at first experienced by Thomas was quickly dispelled by friendships formed in the village. Because he was cheerful, and liked people, doors were readily opened to him. Two families who especially took the youngster to their hearts were the labourers' ones of Giles and Hazlewood. Sons from these homes, respectively Thomas and Joseph, were later to work for Beecham at the farm. Tom Giles had an older sister, Hannah, of whom Thomas was fond, but not romantically.

Chamberlin farmed some four hundred acres. His flocks must

have been considerable, and it was these which Thomas was to inform the editor of *Tit-Bits* he took charge of very early in his teens, and stuck to till he was twenty years of age. As has been seen his employer was a farmer of repute. His trust, therefore, in a mere stripling, and Thomas's justification of such faith, point to the astuteness of the one, and the extreme capability of the other. In time Thomas also came to have charge of the pigs and horses, keeping records of them, together with the years spent caring for the animals, in pencilled scribblings on the walls of his cottage.

Good, or retarding, Thomas was now severed from the influences of an intimate family circle. He was on his own. But the job afforded scope in other ways, too. Banbury, which went back to Saxon times, was a fine town, holding at least a dozen fairs each year. The distant markets Thomas visited in the course of his work, Northampton, Bicester, Oxford and Stratford, all offered variety, and were filled with the bustling crowds he liked. Maturity settled early on him, and soon he was indulging in a few light-hearted affairs.

To sweethearts he was both attractive and baffling. A bit of a dandy, at least when "walking out", and personable, with a small nose, straight brow, and magnetic blue eyes under a thatch of fair hair. Equally hypnotic was his conversation, full of punning wit, a mine of information. Thomas liked to think he knew about everything, and if he did not to give the impression he did. Being employed by exacting Mr. Chamberlin was a recommendation in itself. In contrast, too, to other swains, he drank only moderately at the Brasenose Inn. Very unusual, also, was the fact that he could read and write, and was even a versifier. On the flyleaf of a pocket Bible which bore his signature, and the date 18th April, 1837, and which he consulted so regularly, was written:

> Whithin this awful volume lies
> The Mystery of mysteries;
> Happiest they of human race
> To whom their God has given grace
> To read, to fear, to hope, to pray,
> To lift the hatch, to face the way;
> And better had they ne'er been born
> Who read to doubt or read to scorn.

On the debit side he was eccentric, with a habit of discussing herbs to the point of downright boredom. And he had a disturbingly "dark" side, being nice one moment, nasty the next, and possessing a temper of quite frightening dimensions.

Thomas Beecham—The Old Gentleman

Sarah Morris, Thomas Beecham's mother

Pros and cons apart, however, this rare fish was not to be hooked. If Thomas was ever seriously tempted by a pretty face he had no further to look than his own father for the folly of settling down early to be rammed home to him. Probably he was familiar with the country saying: "When you've got one, you may run, when you've got two you may goo, but when you've got three you must stop where you be." Though ambition was not yet crystallized it certainly did not include remaining where he was indefinitely.

As it happened, in the long run, Oxfordshire was not to figure in his plans at all.

Despite extra duties incurred at The Lawn, shepherding could still drag. Especially on winter evenings, when, after four-thirty, shut into his cottage, Thomas was little more than a super animal minder. Hours could be filled in scratching designs and human figures on the walls. Incredible as it sounds these are still faintly visible today. Thomas also made bobbins and knitting sheaths for his loves. The sheaths were sticks pierced at the top to hold a knitting needle. Worn on the right side in order to release the fingers of the right hand for "throwing" the worsted, and to support the weight of the knitting, they were threaded by means of a carved slot on to a waist belt unceremoniously dubbed a cow band. Sympathetic towards old people Thomas made apple scoopers and pipe stumpers for several in the village. All these items were fashioned with considerable elegance and precision.

Doodlings . . . love tokens . . . these were the recreations of the average shepherd, sometimes with life itself to kill. But that he was no ordinary shepherd Thomas was proving by amateur dabbling and experimenting with herbs. So intense was his enthusiasm in this direction that by his mid-teens he had established a reputation in Cropredy as a curer of all kinds of ailments amongst the locals. With the exception of the astrology, a description in *Folklore* of a nineteenth-century "cunning man" of Essex might, with its blend of sincere quackery and piety, have perfectly applied to Thomas at this period:

"He [Murrell] was a renowned herbalist and animal healer, and as an astrologer was said to be infallible. . . . His cottage was filled with drying herbs which hung in profusion from the ceiling. . . ." Murrell ". . . cultivated an atmosphere of mystery about himself." He was always discussing theological points with the Rector who could never win arguments. " 'He knows his Bible better than I do, said parson. He's either a very good man, or a very bad one, and I can't make up my mind which'." Gentry considered him a dangerous quack, and a disseminator of super-stitious nonsense. But "To the poor he remained to the end a most valuable member of the community, whose magical powers were always at their service. . . ."

As well as human beings Thomas, of course, continued to doctor animals whenever necessary. One day something of tre-mendous import occurred. A horse became ill, Thomas pushed a suitable medicine into its mouth, and it recovered. Nothing unique. He had done it many times before. But either the horse was not expected to get better, or the remedy differed markedly from others, for, as Thomas was to tell a journalist, soon after this he began "making decoctions of a human kind, which was followed by the making of pills . . . sold up and down the country". Eureka! Here *was* the difference. Hitherto his "cures" had been specific; the pill evolved in the cottage was for *general* purposes. By alleviating not one, but many symptoms, it could be offered to the public in the markets after the sheep had been penned, before auctioneering began, and he had leisure to mingle with the crowds. Signposting the way out of farm work it was *the first step towards independence.* The fact hit Thomas with the full force of a cannon ball.

Rooting about in the upper room of Beecham's cottage, Lord Wise, a latter-day tenant, was to find a curious contraption. "A Heath Robinson affair . . . which was obviously used by Beecham to make his pills and mix his herbs, or whatever he put into them. It was a pestle and mortar affair driven by a large wheel taken from some agricultural implement of that time, and the mixture was sent down to the room below by means of a spout which went through a hole in the floor. I decided this affair was Beecham's Mill, and sold it to the firm."

In fact this "mill" was probably only a grinder or kibbler, a piece of barn machinery used for grinding beans for sheep and horses. Additionally, it could have broken down the hard sub-stance of aloes, if bought in block form. Aloes were employed as purges for cows and horses, and also given to sheep as stimu-lants at lambing time. Ginger was another purge, and Thomas incorporated both substances in his pill. Country people liked their doses strong, and internal medicine for humans and animals was to differ very little until 1928. Yet to have used a machine of this size solely for pill-making would have meant having reached the factory stage, and Thomas was only at the domestic stage. Far more significant was the discovery (by someone else) at The Lawn, of a pill board he owned.

Pills, made by hand, undergo three basic stages. Powdered

properties are mixed by pestle and mortar, liquid ingredients added, then small quantities of water, so that a stiff, pliable mass is formed. The mass is converted into pills by rolling on to a marble slab, or grooved board, which also cuts it into strips and squares. Taken off, the pieces are dusted with French chalk to unsticky them, then shaped—either by rolling again on the board, or between the palms in a slow, rhythmic figure of eight movement. They are then left to dry for several weeks before, if one is given, receiving a coating. Thomas always preferred to finish off his pills by hand. His long fingers were ideally suited for the task, and people watching them revolve up and round, and down and round again in unbroken motion were fascinated. Sometimes he rolled his pills absent-mindedly when carrying on a conversation, much as a painter licks his brush.

His Cropredy pill, naturally, was crude, only a forerunner of his celebrated "herbal" or costive one, which he was to spend many years altering and perfecting.

In 1838 William Hunt Chamberlin, now past sixty and with thoughts of retirement, bought a house in the nearby village of Adderbury. Adderbury House has belonged successively to the Earls of Rochester, the Duke of Argyle, and the Duke of Buccleugh. Though by now scaled down to the "dimensions of a commodious modern mansion", the property was still imposing. Chamberlin went to live there that year, or the next one, but continued as tenant of the Lawn Farm until about 1849.

New brooms sweep clean. On the whole Thomas's stay in Cropredy had been felicitous. He was well thought of, had made many friends. But at twenty he had had more than enough of shepherding, and a fresh master, even one in a bailiff capacity, was a spur to quit. Chamberlin was a man of taste. Watching the transfer of his numerous belongings, books, maps, china and pictures to a still larger building which included a Green Room as well as a library, it was impossible not to contrast, adversely, the lot of employee with employer. The stark fact was, farming paid, labouring did not. Thomas had been twelve grinding years at the job, yet would be no nearer to owning a roomful of furniture in a dozen more unless he changed his mode of work.

In leaving Cropredy in 1840 was he galvanized by a greater urge than envy? By optimism—or even good luck? What was "the slight turn in the tide of events" which made him feel ready to launch his "tiny barque on the ever-shifting sea of commercial uncertainty"? Was it merely the discovery of a pill formula which promised him independence, or had a grateful master adequately rewarded a good worker? Chamberlin was known to be generous. In his will two servants were to benefit by annuities. Shepherds also received extra money at lambing time, and Thomas may well have salted away a tidy sum. Whatever the reasons, Thomas felt sufficiently confident to strike out on his own.

A great deal had happened since he had first gone to The Lawn Farm. Then he had been a homesick youngster with only three or four years' shepherding experience behind him, much of it supervised. Now he was a man who had acquitted himself admirably in a position of trust, who had made his mark in a strange village, whom God obviously favoured, and with those whose help he was capable of steering his own destiny. Life bubbled with hope.

Meanwhile, the outside world had not been standing still, either.

By now Queen Victoria sat on the throne. Banbury had celebrated her coronation on a balmy day in 1837 with an idyllic procession of woolcombers, weavers and gardeners led by a picaresque shepherd and shepherdess with a dog and lamb, as far removed from grim reality as Adderbury House from "Beecham's cottage". The following year the London to Birmingham railway had been opened up. Since then the country had gone railroad mad. Hundreds of acts authorizing new lines had been passed, the age of steam driven machinery had arrived with a vengeance. More quietly, but as revolutionary in scope, the penny post had been introduced in 1839.

Nearer home a second brother William, born in 1835, and a new sister Ann, arriving two years later, had completed Joseph Beecham's family. And on 1st March, 1839, Joseph himself died aged forty. His death, following the rupture of a blood vessel, was so sudden that an inquest was ordered. At it the coroner, plainly puzzled, returned the quaint verdict that Joseph had "died by the visitation of God".

According to Thomas his parents had not got on, and towards the end his father had taken up a different abode in Curbridge. It seems improbable that Joseph, who found the burden of one household too much, could have supported two. What is just as unlikely, however, is that, given the circumstances and the period in which they lived, the couple could ever have enjoyed much domestic happiness.

4

# ITINERANT PEDLAR

THOMAS, when he left Cropredy, had no actual sense of vocation. He desired to be independent, rid forever of farm work; beyond that the future glimmered promising, but obscure. Though long since weaned from the little grey stone cottage, even had he wished to return there overcrowding would have made this impracticable. Only sister Mary was away in domestic service. All the others were at home. Beside, a cloud darkened the household.

On 20th September, 1840, Thomas's mother, Sarah, had remarried. Her new bridegroom was Thomas Morris, a local labourer. A girl, Elizabeth was born the following January, and two more children were to result from the union. Another daughter, Fanny, and a son, Charles, born on Christmas Day 1848 when Sarah was as old as the century, a factor which stresses her extreme hardihood.

If Sarah considered herself fortunate to marry again in middle age, with the youngest of her seven children still a toddler, she had frequent cause to change her mind. Morris, who drank deep and hard, was also vicious in his cups, and at forty-two too old to mend his ways. Rolling home from the Merry Horn, or the Herd and Swine, rows would ensue, ornaments and chairs be sent flying. The younger children were particularly frightened, and often took refuge under a table.

So it was to Kidlington, a village about six miles from Oxford, instead of Curbridge, that Thomas went, after scraping the mud from the Lawn Farm off his boots. Apart from the fact that it sent thousands of apricots yearly to Covent Garden, and the church choir sang to the accompaniment of a clarionet, bassoon, violincello, and other instruments, Kidlington was insignificant. It was without a railway, while, due to the enclosure of the common land completed by 1820 "both sheep and shepherds were miserably poor", as Arthur Young had noted in a report. Since Thomas was lively his sole reason for going there was because it was here that his uncle, William Beecham, had settled after leaving home.

Uncle William, it may be remembered, was a shepherd. When

his wife had died as far back as 1827 he had quickly consoled himself with a seventeen-year-old bride. At this time his household included Henry, aged eighteen, a son by his first marriage, and Job, thirteen, by his second, and a labourer. Like his cousin Thomas, Henry was nimble with his fingers. A stick lodged today in Reading Rural Museum, dated 1844-9 and executed by "Henry Beecham, a poor shepherd of Kidlington" is undoubtedly his handiwork. Beautifully engraved, faces are carved from notches in the wood, one of Christ being almost Byzantine in conception. Exhortations on it, however, to "Live as you would wish to die", and "Our blessed Saviour dying for us and we must pray to him to save us" contrast so sharply with the frivolity of a walking stick made by Thomas and dated 1840, that they help to explain why Henry, with his obvious gifts, faded into limbo, whereas Thomas made a success of life. A saying in the family had it that there was nothing sadder than a sad Beecham, sadness being synonymous with failure. Thomas's own stick is worth a second mention. In the form of a hieroglyphic love letter, he begs his sweetheart to meet him at church on the 22nd day of May. Drawn in considerable detail the church closely resembles that at nearby Deddington, where some distant Beecham relations lived. No marriage took place, of course, Thomas still sliding in and out of romances, but the stick was an obvious *pièce de résistance*, for he kept it all his life. The amount of work crammed on to it is quite fantastic. Besides the message to the unknown girl Thomas engraved Biblical quotations and figures. Of especial interest is a skeletal, though jaunty, figure of death, the same which accompanied wool burial certificates in the seventeenth century, when, to help the trade, corpses had to be wrapped in a woollen shroud.

At first Thomas stayed with his uncle in the Beecham's sand-and-stone cottage on the green. Three-roomed, it had a small garden in front, with a field behind. Here Thomas pounded and rolled his pills so enthusiastically that the cottage came to be known as the "Pill House". He went around collecting herbs from meadows and hedges which he stuffed into a little sack. Dandelion root was a favourite. According to *The English Physician Enlarged*, a work on plants which Thomas studied assiduously, this root had an opening and cleaning quality, being very effectual, among other things, for relieving obstructions of the liver, gall, and spleen. It also went by the crude title of Pis-a-beds. "A bit of a quack, but one of good repute," was the local verdict on this young nephew of William Beecham's, normal in every respect except for his strange *penchant* for matters medical.

Thomas was obliged to supplement his income by casual work, obtaining the job of postman, or letter carrier as it was then called. Kidlington lacking a post office, the mail was collected from a cottage at Gosford, Thomas placing it in an envelope-shaped bag. In the evenings he blew a horn at certain points of the village, and people ran from their houses handing him letters for dispatch. Thus he was a walking pillar box, though that article was not then in use. At this date, too, uniforms were not worn in provincial offices, but Thomas's thick farm clothes were more than adequate.

Either letter carrying was not sufficiently remunerative, or Thomas decided to engage in other work as well, for he became jobbing gardener to a Mr. John Pudsey Welchman Sydenham at Hampden House, once Hampden Manor, at Mill End. About the same time he moved to a cottage opposite his place of employment.

Hampden House was steeped in history. Tradition has it that it was here, during the Civil War, the incident occurred which inspired W. F. Yeames' famous picture where a child royalist, confronted by officers of the Roundhead army, is asked where he last saw his father. Sydenham, Thomas's new employer, was a bachelor with the independent turn of mind Thomas admired. He had been against the enclosure acts, feeling convinced that the introduction of machinery into agriculture both ruined the yeoman farmer, and caused local unemployment. Though no "Swing" riots had taken place in Kidlington, Sydenham nevertheless played a compassionate rôle in them. Puffing on a churchwarden in his cosy parlour he helped organize rebellions in the neighbourhood, and personally composed letters to farmers. For this he was obliged to pay heavy fines, and a large part of his property was confiscated, but needless to say he was very popular in the village amongst the labourers.

For the job Thomas wore bright blue overalls. Meanwhile he continued to busy himself with pestle and mortar in his spare moments, making use of an ornamental water closet in the garden. Local legend has it that one day he noticed that animals chewed curatively in the field behind his uncle's cottage. Plucking some of the grasses there, Thomas idly rolled them with a piece of soap in his pocket, and so produced a pill which he swallowed with aperient effect. He mentioned this to a doctor "who lived in Hampden House", and together they manufactured a pill which was given to the doctor's patients. Rushing in from his rounds the doctor would shout to Thomas to let him have several more dozen pills, then dash off again on his errands of mercy. Later, cart-loads of the grass were said to be driven to St. Helens when Thomas came to have a factory there!

Wild as the story is, it does contain a germ of credibility. Chemist's soap was incorporated in Thomas's costive pill. And although employer Sydenham was a gentleman of leisure, and not a doctor, a licensed apothecary of the same name did live at Moor End, where Thomas also stayed. In 1841 this doctor was twenty-eight. Sydenham, then nearly fifty, had a natural son, who was to reside and die at Islip. John Pudsey Welchman Sydenham the *doctor* later transferred from Kidlington to Islip, dying there. The coincidence of the name makes it impossible not to suppose that the latter was not Sydenham's natural son. But even if this was untrue, as the only qualified doctor in the village Thomas would certainly have met him. Whilst the fact that his pill, especially in its embryo stage, received professional approval, must have been highly rewarding.

Many other stories were to spring up regarding the pill's origin. Some, like the grass one, are worth quoting. A grateful gypsy to whom he did a good turn is said to have given Thomas the formula. Once, when a young man, he became indisposed. The doctor whom he consulted dosed him with a pill which proved so effective that Thomas requested, and was supplied with, the recipe. Again, his mother is supposed to have made it first, passing on her knowledge to her son. And a variation of this: everyone in Curbridge possessed the formula, only Thomas had the perspicacity to market it.

By far the most lurid, and my favourite, concerns a shepherd Thomas had worked for at Curbridge. This shepherd showed Thomas how to make the pill, and extracted a promise from him that he would later commercialize it for his wife. When it became evident that Thomas was using it for his own advantage, and that he had been cheated, the shepherd summoned Beecham to his deathbed, and cursed him to the third and fourth generation.

Thomas's only public mention of how he came to evolve his pill is that given in the preceding chapter, and must thus be accepted as the correct one.

Inevitably, and in due course, Kidlington palled. It was too unimportant, too circumscribed, for Thomas's smouldering ambitions. Moreover, employed as a jobbing gardener, he was in as much danger of vegetating as he had been at Cropredy. So he became an itinerant pedlar, selling his pills and cures, which he carried in a pack, in villages and markets. He had various addresses, including a room which he rented in a dwelling house in Corn Street, Witney. It was often a desperate existence, as some lines engraved on a staff worked between 1842-3 suggest. "Reader. If you will you may succeed in wonderful things. Don't say 'I can't', he is a scamp: Can't has ruin'd many a man. Look up! Try again. For where there's 'a will' there's a way'." Thomas continued this handwork, partly from habit, but mostly because he enjoyed doing it, and enforced idleness of any kind irked him. A wooden crook worked on the following year shows that he was still composing, or recording doggerel.

> Youth is the time would you be blest,
> With God's peculiar smile
> The time the most approved and best
> To learn his sovereign will
> Tis the sweet morning of your days
> When reason's dawn appears
> If spent in sacred Wisdom's ways
> Twill crown your future years.

Thomas occasionally sold his wares to shops. For a while a woman in West End, Witney, who kept a "shop-house" included them for display along with her sweets, salves and simples. Eventually, however, she discouraged Thomas's visits, "not thinking much of him, as he was a great womanizer". His amorous nature was already becoming notorious, and scandals were to pursue him well into old age. Thomas also tried to interest chemists in his products, but they proved obstinate customers, preferring to push their own, or well-known brands. A few, no doubt pitying the youthful vendor, placed some of his pills on their shelves. But weeks later, when Thomas returned to renew stocks, it was only to find that the old ones had not been touched, but were still gathering dust where they had been put. He had much better luck in the markets which he liked, being a natural orator. The difficulty, in fact, was not so much to *draw* crowds, as to *hold* them. When he had done with the patter, had got down to brass tacks, when it became a matter of parting the country-man from his money, someone was sure to shrug, turn away. Like silly sheep the rest would follow suit. Impossible to be amongst them fast enough! An assistant was necessary. Some-one who could start raking in the pennies while Thomas was still speaking. He was found. And speedily discarded.

In October, 1846, Thomas's second oldest sister Mary married a labourer, William Carvey. Twenty-one, Carvey had good looks, charm, and a breezy personality. Ostensibly he seemed just the man to win the confidence of women who constituted the bulk of the market buyers, wheedle money from their tightly clasped purses. With a dazzling dream of easy living, Carvey eagerly entered into a partnership, helping Thomas roll the pills in a cottage at Bampton, the village where he and Mary first settled. Alas, for all his virtues, Carvey had a besetting sin. His earnings melted away all too easily in the inns. Thomas had seen enough of the evils of alcohol at close quarters ever to trust an habitual drinker. Soon he was on his own again.

He was growing despondent. Six years had passed since he had left the Lawn Farm, yet he had made no real progress. The lives of the here-today-gone-tomorrow men which had so enchanted him as a child, were, when emulated, singularly unromantic. Thomas was often as hungry, too, as he had been in his early farming days. Expecting so much from her firstborn, by far the cleverest and most intelligent, his mother was sorely puzzled. Thomas seemed content to waste his gifts in a nomad life, instead of doing the sensible thing of settling down and earning a steady living. Both his brothers were now labourers, whilst at Thomas's own age his father had been supporting a wife and three children. And irritatingly, setting another good example, was Tom Templer, who four years ago had married his cousin Leah Beecham, had a small boy, and a regular job on a farm.

Templer, as it happened, was Thomas's biggest argument for not being "sensible". The former, known as the scholar of Curbridge, composed music in his leisure, read and wrote letters for parents whose children had emigrated, and still talked loftily of leaving the country himself. But he was stuck in a menial rut without any visible prospects of being able to achieve his aim. Better to persevere, better even to go under, than return to hated agricultural employment again! But it was far from easy. A constant worry was his poor health. The distances to the various markets from wherever he might be based—to Abingdon, Oxford, or Banbury, were not onerous for an ex-shepherd. They were however, to a pedlar carrying a pack sometimes twenty miles there and back on an empty belly. Occasionally Thomas fainted from sheer fatigue. He tended to get light-headed. Too often he seemed to be outside his body, goading it forward like a reluctant animal. Once he fainted in a ditch and nearly drowned. Another time he was trudging along a country road when he heard a voice seeming to come from the other side of the hedge. "One day," it said, "you will ride in your own carriage." Thinking someone was playing a joke on him, Thomas peered over the hedge, but nobody was behind it. He grew very excited, supposing it to have been a divine utterance. It was the supreme moment of his life. To ride in a personally owned carriage was still the sum total of ambition. Now he *knew* it would be fulfilled!

Thomas's spirits were quickly restored by this episode, peddling was continued to such good effect that, by the end of the year, or early the next, he had made sufficient money to go north. The idea had been at the back of his mind for some time, the drift being very favoured amongst labourers in the southern villages, pay being higher there since competition engendered by the proximity of mines and factories served to keep up rural wages. Thomas either worked his way to Lancashire, or went directly, for by the spring of 1847, and possibly for several months previously, he was living in Liverpool.

His targets were always comparatively modest, and at this period were no more grandiose than those of other men of his class who were taking the drastic step of tearing up roots. In short, they were to lift himself and his family from the degrading trough of poverty, to establish independence, and then, one fine day, return to his birth-place, the prodigal whose gamble had paid off.

Except that Thomas was to leave the north for only a relatively brief interval, the plan succeeded formidably. While, had he known the exact size of the fortune he was to coin it would have seemed a hundred times more startling than the voice which had addressed him so commandingly behind the hedge.

PART TWO

# THE NORTH

# 5

# MARRIAGE

FAR from being paved with gold, Liverpool streets, as Thomas quickly discovered, could be as unlucrative as Oxfordshire lanes. Again he was obliged to seek casual work on outlying farms, and also in the building trade. Meanwhile, midnight oil continued to be burnt making pills which he sold in the evening in Whitechapel. Here, gas flowing from enormous jets, illuminated the various booths in the narrow street where pawnshops abounded, herb doctors and chiropodists fiercely out-shouted each other. Thomas's lodgings were hard by in Circus Street, since pulled down, but then a seedy thoroughfare seldom mentioned in directories. The house was one of several unwieldy, red-brick buildings, once privately owned, but now let out into rooms which often included whole families, slumdom having successfully driven away the middle classes.

Conditions in the city were, in fact, among the worst in England at that time, the root cause being cholera, which had first broken out some twelve years earlier. Liverpool had become a world port, and inevitably sailors and immigrants brought disease in their wake. Matters had worsened in 1846 when the potato famine in Ireland had resulted in a great exodus. Leaving the country at the rate of 250,000 a year the refugees, usually verminous and filthy from travelling as deck cargo on cattle ships, descended on Liverpool. So shattered was he by what he saw that Charles Dickens, roaming the docks in search of material, was to aid with his pen the social revolution in the middle years of the century, much as Kingsley's would later help boy chimney sweeps.

For some reason Circus Street was popular with Welsh settlers, and it was in the same road, perhaps in the same house, that Thomas met the woman who was to be his first wife. Jane Evans was "Liverpool Welsh" having left her native Bangor some years before in company with her father, a labourer. She was employed as maid to a chemist. The match was one of convenience on both sides, rather than passion, since the couple were singularly ill-suited. Years afterwards Thomas was to declare he had only been in love once in his life, and he made it clear it was not with Jane. Unable to write, possibly wholly illiterate, she had a fine singing voice, a dour personality, and was subject to fits of neurosis. Thomas, with his bad temper, and who could be impatient with illness, was hardly the calm companion she needed. But, nearly eight years his senior, Jane wanted to settle down. And Thomas himself was only too well aware of his own necessity for doing so. A rolling stone gathers no moss. Just so long as he combined pill-making with odd jobs, so long would any hope of a proper career go on being delayed. He, too, was anxious to start a family, and often homesick. The older woman may well have been a substitute Sarah whom he missed enormously.

They were married in Liverpool Parish Church on 26th May, 1847. Witnesses were a female relation of the bride's, and a male shop-keeping friend of the groom's. A labourer was how Thomas described his occupation in the register. Never again was he to give this definition. For hand-in-glove with marriage went the vital decision to become a full-time medicine vendor. Liverpool, with its terrible poverty, was no good for trade, and during the summer Thomas and his new wife moved to Wallgate in Wigan. Wallgate was the address given on a medicine licence stamped 1st September, 1847. It was essential to have one. Till now, since he was peddling pills by pack, the law had not required it, but if he intended packaging his articles, or laying claim to a unique recipe, both of which he did, it was impossible to avoid paying a stamp duty.

In selecting Wigan, Thomas was influenced primarily by the fact that the town was in a flourishing state. For the men the chief occupations were the mines and heavy engineering, for the women the mills, and all three industries thrived. It was also ideally situated. The railway, the third passenger one to be opened in England, had connections with Manchester, Preston, Liverpool and Birmingham. Business for Thomas depending on the markets, important market towns such as Bolton, Chorley, and Ormskirk were in easy reach, whilst within a twenty-mile radius were Salford, Warrington, Rochdale and Bury. If, on the obverse side, Wigan had a hundred and thirty taverns and public houses, it could also boast three coffee and temperance houses, a savings bank and Mechanics Institute, while the streets, unlike those in many large towns, were well lit by gas.

The Beechams settled in the Wiend, a cobbled alley near the market place. Close by was the parish church of All Saints, and,

Thomas's three sisters: (*above left*) Jane; (*above right*) Mary; (*right*) Ann

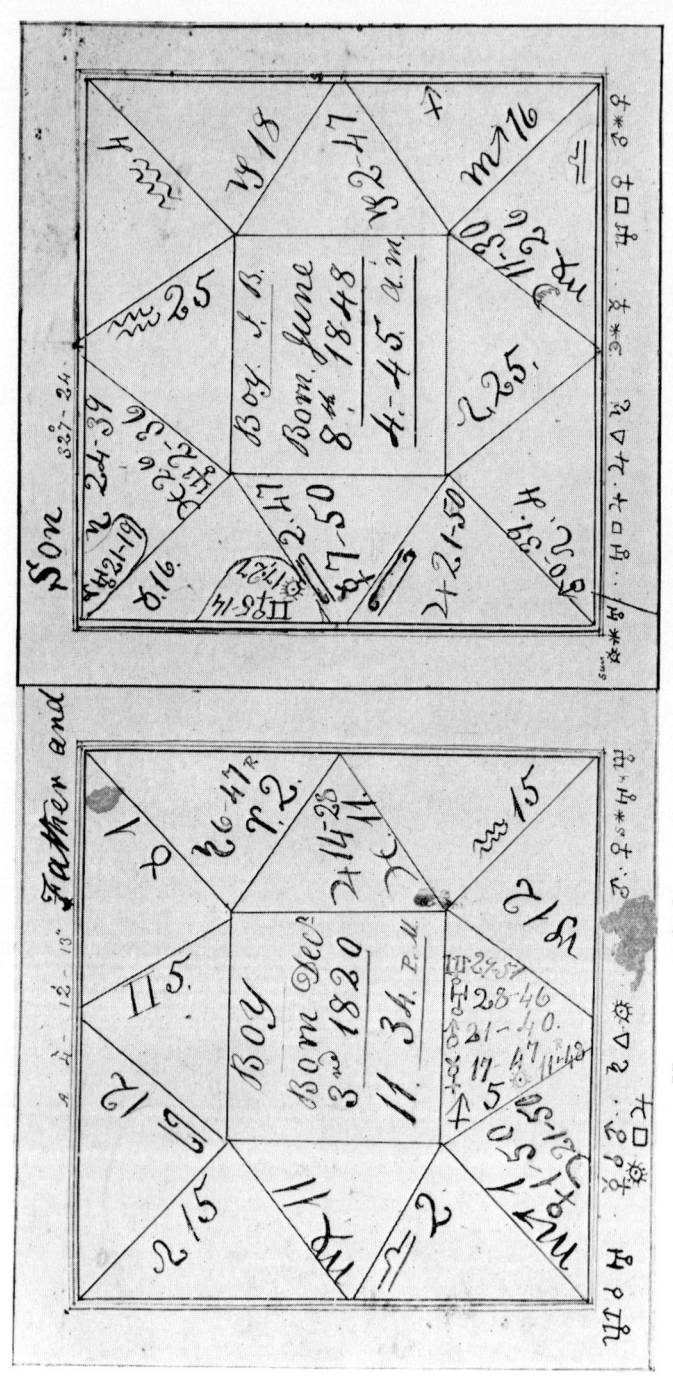

Horoscopes of Thomas Beecham and his son Joseph, as cast by himself

counteracting the puritan chill it cast, the inns of the Red Lion
and the Three Tuns. Their neighbours were minor trades people,
shoemakers and commercial travellers. Wigan itself, with its
red slate roofs and intimate clog-and-shawl atmosphere, was a
refreshing change from the dirt and cosmopolitanism of Liverpool. If sleepy villages caused Thomas's feet to tap, cities with
their anonymity also made him ill at ease, and in this busy, yet
domestic atmosphere, he felt at home. Amongst Lancastrians he
was completely relaxed. Though born in the south his affinity
lay unmistakeably in the north. There was no period of orienta-
tion; from the start he *belonged*. He had the Oxfordshire man's
punning wit, but his brusqueness, wry tongue, zeal, and common
sense attitude were wholly northern.

Indifferent to anyone else's comfort, Thomas, at the manual
stage of pill-making, always monopolized the largest, and so
usually best, room in his home. Records of sales were scribbled
on the walls, as once at Cropredy numbers of lambs weaned and
animals cared for, had been jotted down.

At this stage he marketed four products. The first was the costive pill evolved in Oxfordshire, which mysteriously, and for many
years to come, he called "herbal" long after it contained no herbs
whatsoever. It was sold in wooden boxes at 1s. 6d. each; a
government stamp was attached to every box, together with a
red and yellow label bearing his name and place of operation. A
pill vaguely styled "Female's Friend", a "Royal Toothpowder"
retailed at fourpence a box, and a "Golden Tooth Tincture" completed his stock-in-trade.

A stickler for routine Thomas now devised a system which
served him for several decades. Once a week he mixed, and made
up the pills. The rest of the time was devoted to hawking them
round the markets, and attending to desk work entailed. The
actual "mixing" of his costive pill—the formation of solids and
liquids into a pill mass, a process already described, was kept a
close secret. Several proprietary brands of the day were, broadly
speaking, compounded of similar ingredients. Success lay as much
as anything in the exact *balance* of the components achieved,
and it was this which, in the main, was so jealously guarded.
(Thomas's own proportions were so perfect that future chemists
at the firm were to try in vain to improve on them).

He still walked vast distances, at first being too poor to go
much by train, though now instead of a pack he carried a
basket. Inside it, an invincible warning, bumped a bottle of
worms. His audiences had concrete evidence of what would hap-
pen to them if they did not swallow his wares. And as he talked

D

on they would feel discomfited, anyway, that the worst had already befallen them. Occasional help was employed for the selling, usually young boys he did not have to give much to. When Thomas came to have handbills printed, they preceded him through the towns, scattering them in shops and hedgerows, much the same way that the little Thomas had seen circus hands do in the south. These bills were printed in vivid colours to attract attention, oranges, greens and yellows.

Dispensing with a stall, at first financially out of the question, Thomas's market equipment included a bamboo table with, on wet days, a vast umbrella, possibly a shepherd's gig he had brought north. Like most other market towns Wigan had its full quota of her doctors and quacks, whilst representatives of pill firms posted themselves at given spots on specific days. More pill vendors turned up at the fairs, rubbing shoulders with pickpockets, gypsies, and hard-and-sharp men from Sheffield, who "gave away" pocket knives for sixpence, and lived in gaudy caravans. Thomas's assets in so much competition were his blazing sincerity and remarkable powers of persuasion. He passionately believed in his products. Herbs were a whole way of life, and as such sacrosanct. In the sense that he did not adapt himself to people, he was no actor. What he was, he was to everyone encountered, whether a client or friend. And his honesty, in a county which prided itself on this trait, came across far more powerfully than any smooth ways would have done. "He was a wonderful salesman," an elderly Wiganite remembers his grandfather telling him. "He could have sold anything he wanted to. People, when they began listening to him, might feel fit enough. But after a time their backs began aching, then their stomachs, and limbs. When Beecham had finally finished they felt so queasy they were only too glad to buy his medicines."

Thomas's voice has been described by those who heard it as being "thunderous", and also, "a bit on the light side". The truth is probably somewhere in between. It was both resonant, and, despite a native burr, distinct. His Oxfordshire brogue, which he always retained, stamped him out more than anything else, as a "foreigner". At first the townspeople did not mind this, but later, the fact he was a stranger would be remembered and recorded against him. Like his everyday utterances Thomas's patter was a mixture of hard fact and Biblical allusion, for he had stayed deeply religious. Hailing from a part of the country where the sayings of the people were rich in imagery, to this inheritance he added the poet's natural inversion of words, plus a sharp tongue. Interpolators were speedily and effectively put in their places. When Thomas was around, particularly when he was selling, there was only one opinion which counted—his.

Scrupulously clean on the job, pill board, pestle and mortar were kept in immaculate condition. He was now supremely happy. For at last he was his own master, working the markets he loved. His energy was boundless. He toiled from early morning till far into the night, mixing pills, pounding tinctures, tramping between the towns. Totally engrossed, he failed to notice, or did not deem it important, that Jane was insufficiently occupied. Hers was an inward looking nature which needed to be constantly absorbed. Cleaning a small home took up very little time. Cooking, too, for Thomas, for whom meals were as often as not an intrusion instead of a necessity, was discouraging. Besides, he would be away for days on end, which made her restive. A solution to boredom, as well as frustration, could always be found in the parlours of the Three Tuns, or the Red Lion. They were warm, filled with congenial company. Easy to make a habit of them. In time, too easy. . . .

By the early summer of the following year, however, Jane had something personal with which to occupy her mind. This was their first child.

Fair-haired, grey-eyed, the baby was born at 4.45 a.m. 8th June, 1848, and christened Joseph at the parish church. Thomas duly entered the event in the flyleaf of a massive family Bible. He also plotted his own, and his son's, nativity. Readers with any knowledge on the subject may care to work these out for themselves, whilst the findings of two experts, X and Y, are interesting. Neither, of course, knew the identities of the subjects at the time of examining the nativities.

Using the sidereal Zodiac, X thought that Thomas, employing the Tropical, had assumed he was a Saggitarian, whereas "his Sun was really in the sidereal sign of Scorpio". This, together with X's interpretation of the positions of the planets at the time of his birth, made Thomas a man of great gifts, personality, and one whom it would have been difficult to persuade to alter his opinion, or attitude to life. Strong-willed, "he would always think he was right, and would pay little regard to other's principles, or points of view." He would have mathematical ability, scientific interests, a complex temperament, and be basically versatile. His character would have been considerably influenced by family ties persisting throughout his life, also by early background and environment.

Career-wise, X considered something fairly important would

have happened to Thomas at the age of eight, again at twenty, whilst in his mid-thirties he would have been tempted to speculate. But the outstanding part of his career would have been in his fortieth year, when he would have made a significant move. Prosperity would be his, also disputes and legislations.

So far, so true. Thomas's character is well depicted. Early environment certainly moulded his life, throughout which he remained extremely attached to the Oxfordshire Beechams. The important event at the age of eight can be interpreted as going to work. Latish in his thirties he was to make a short-termed business venture, whilst some months before turning forty he would dramatically leave Wigan.

Supporting much of this, Y has thought that a professional interest might have included farming, or an agricultural pursuit. Both astrologists have curiously erred in reading a "good marriage" into Thomas's nativity, good in the sense it would bring him money, or be connected with position. However, Y has been nearer the mark in finding that a dual sign on the cusp of the marriage house implied more than one marriage.

Regarding Joseph's nativity both X and Y have been in complete agreement that he "was a very clever man with much negotiation and financial skills, and good at mathematics". X has attributed a love of music to him, and a liking for the grand life. "At the age of fifty-six he would have been heaped with public honours," but before this "would have carved a successful career for himself in medicine, and would have travelled widely." Joseph's, X has maintained, was essentially the horoscope of a person who would have had an impersonal approach to life rather than a warmly affectionate or emotional one. As it happened, Joseph never cared to, or was incapable of, displaying his feelings, and has been accused of indifference, even heartlessness, by members of his family.

X and Y have again jointly slipped up in giving Joseph the greater chance of longevity. The father it was who would live to a ripe old age, whilst the son would die suddenly, nine years later, and soon after the last of the public honours had been bestowed on him.

Thomas's interest in astrology had a slightly macabre origin, and helps to illustrate the "dark" side of his nature. At this time he was in the habit of consulting a white witch in the Midlands. Warned that his temper would land him in serious trouble if he did not make greater efforts to control it, shortly after this, and in a heated argument with Jane, he began kicking her with his boots. Just in time he remembered the prophecy, and restrained himself. He was so impressed that there and then astrology became a consuming hobby. The incident also shows how quickly his marriage had begun to deteriorate.

Accolades, financial security, and legal disputes were still far off in the future. Meanwhile, it had become important to find a new home. A baby, especially with Thomas commandeering the best room and locking himself into it for hours together, made the Wiend lodgings too cramped. By the time a daughter, Sarah Ann, had arrived in 1850, the Beechams had moved to Hallgate, a different part of the town. Oddly, the little girl was born at the exact hour of her brother. Thomas must have cast her nativity, but since she was to grow up as dreamy and undistinguished as Joseph was to be astute and successful, perhaps he did not think it worth preserving.

Hallgate houses were the depressing tenement kind so typical of the industrial north. Two up and two down, many had been homes of the servants of the Hall, or labourers working on parson's land. Fortunately the Beechams were not to stay there long, for by July 1851 they had moved again, to No. 6 New Square, Standishgate. Either the numbers of these houses became changed, or this residence was only makeshift, for by the following year the family was installed at No. 7, today No. 8. The rateable value was £5 15s. od. and Thomas's name was to appear there continuously on the town rate books for the next five years.

The new home though small, with only two bedrooms, a living-room and scullery, had several advantages. The alley opened directly on to the market, thus simplifying transport of the bamboo table. It had a cellar, into the beams of which Thomas drove hooks to suspend his herbs, and here he could work uninterrupted. He hated to be disturbed. "Nit-wit!" and "Shut your row!" were ephithets shouted at offenders. A tiny yard at the back was useful for hanging out washing, or bundling the children into. Despite lack of space the Beechams managed to accommodate a youthful maid who went by the Dickensian name of Alice Tickle. Here Jane's remaining children were born. An especially cherished daughter called after her, in February 1853, and William in August 1855. Each was baptised at All Saints, their names solemnly entered in ink in the family Bible.

Though determined to stay independent, Thomas was still uncertain of his ultimate goal. Indecision is reflected by the various titles he adopted at this period: "Quack Doctor," "Worm Doctor," "Medicine Vendor". He was also offering his customers

additional attractions. "A never failing remedy for Deafness provided the ear of the drum is not broken, and as a "Student of
Physick and the Celestial Sciences," he preferred help of another
nature. On a handout which bore his name and address—T.
Beecham, Near the Savings Bank—and below the optimistic
caption: HOPE LEADS US ON, Mr. Beecham begged to inform
"Ladies and Gentlemen who may feel disposed to consult him
that he will calculate their Nativity, from which is given a correct
judgment, pointing out the Mental Qualities, Disposition, Constitutional Diseases, the employment or Profession for which
persons are best adapted, the time of Marriage, with a description
of the Wife or Husband, and whether likely to marry more than
once. Enemies and all the general affairs of life until Death. Also
Honrary inquiries or questions answered; if debts will be paid,
and whether it is safe to go on a journey or not."

A poor speller, by "honrary" Thomas must have meant horary,
a time measurement. How easy and touching to envisage the trek
along the cobbled alley! The cap or bonnet pulled closer about
the face to dodge prying eyes, the shawl tightened. Then the
surreptitious knock at the front door. Jane answering, perhaps,
irritably shooing the children from the living-room. Or, if
Thomas was not mixing, futures might be told, auras diagnosed,
in the basement. According to their temperaments, problems, and
sex, individuals would be cowed, flattered, or palpably alarmed
by Thomas's Rabelaisian personality. Hypnotised into still-
ness by the burning blue eyes and the somnolent figure of eight
movement as a pill was rolled and rolled between the long
fingers.

How facilely, also, the inhabitants of a small town of that era
are conjured up! Constitutional diseases. . . . Fevers, the Victorian
plague, engendered by inadequate sanitation, and consumption,
often brought on by long hours and bad conditions in factories.
And visiting relations by train. . . . Was it *really* urgent, when
*Punch* was so grimly amusing about this still-novel mode of
travelling? "Every passenger in the second or third class is to
be allowed to carry a dark lantern, or a penny candle. . . . The
ladies' carriages are to be waited upon by female policemen."
Debts incurred were doubtless due to large families, whilst
"Enemies" to be dealt with hints at petty feuds induced by a
confined society. If the Student of Physick had a large clientele
his insight into his neighbours' lives must have been as detailed,
and dangerous, as that of the "cunning man", Murrell, who
had ". . . maintained a remarkable intelligence system which
kept him briefed of all local affairs." By judicious questioning he

would "pump" those who consulted him, note and file information. In due course knowledge would be disclosed to other clients with devastating effect.

Thomas was making steady headway. Easing of finances meant that Curbridge could be visited at least once a year, and pleasure combined with business; local shops and chemists, now more amenable, be approached, even London markets be explored.

Sister Jane was married, otherwise the little grey stone cottage was as full as ever. Besides Thomas's stepfather, and Granny Morris, as Sarah was now known, were sister Ann, the two half-sisters, and the half-brother Charles, only slightly younger than Thomas's own Joseph. Although living so far away, "Our Tom" had constituted himself undisputed leader of the clan. His arrival would be the scene of a great get-together of the gregarious Beechams. The walls echoed with noise as everyone talked, laughed, and gesticulated all at once, Thomas's voice managing to ride the hub-bub like a giant wave crashing down over smaller ones. His tales of the bustling north were, to these slower-moving southerners, as bizarre as if he spoke of foreign parts; whilst he, the countryman at heart, would listen avidly to farm gossip. After the years spent peddling in local lanes it was comforting to be so obviously making good. To boss, heckle, advise, scold them all. Then, before leaving, sweep them off for a slap-up meal at the Merry Horn whose rear windows overlooked the downs where, a half-starved boy, he had tended sheep. Even more rewarding, since he was generosity incarnate, was it to shower them with gifts. Presents took a practical turn, were blankets, dress lengths, sovereigns, and gorgeously coloured sweets for the younger children. Having come up the hard way Thomas knew how to spoil, and he never bought cheaply. The frocks fashioned for the half-sisters from the material given them were of such durable cloth that they were eventually cut up and stitched into a patchwork cot cover, still in the family today, and in excellent condition.

Two people who heard out Thomas's exploits with particular interest were his brother-in-law, Carvey, and cousin, Tom Templer. Carvey kicked himself for lost opportunity. Late he went north and begged Thomas to re-employ him. Thomas refused. Carvey still drank. Eventually he became a shepherd and carter, but though a heavy drinker all his life, the vice had no serious effects, since he died at the huge age of ninety! Templer had stayed a labourer, but, spurred on by Thomas's example, as Thomas had been by his earlier on, he achieved his ambition of emigrating a few years later. The voyage to South Africa was made by sailing ship. It took three months and was so ghastly that some of the passengers sent up prayers for the boat to sink. As it transpired, the Templers lost a baby at sea. Tragically, Templer's mother never saw the faith she had placed in her son justified, having died in 1847.

Granny Morris does not seem to have journied north to see for herself the curious speaking people and towns of Thomas's outpourings. To the end of her days she remained a simple cottager, absorbed and content with the small change of village life. It was difficult for the married sisters to leave their homes, but occasionally Ann travelled back to Wigan with her brother. Jane's health was now so unsatisfactory that, despite the services of her maid, she often found herself unable to cope with the household chores. Ann helped with the children.

At first Ann enjoyed these visits. She was Thomas's favourite sister, and he made a great fuss of her. But soon joy was marred. Jane resented her presence. Quarrels could be as bitter as those at Curbridge. There was an ugly incident in which Jane slammed a window on her sister-in-law's hand whilst the latter was nursing a child. After a time Ann's visits stopped altogether. In 1855, when still under age, she married a man considerably older than herself. He was a carpenter and undertaker and the match promised well. Unhappily though, like Carvey, he too was addicted to the bottle, and when the family ran into money trouble Thomas unselfishly aided them.

In fairness, Jane had reason to feel peeved. It was paradoxical that whereas Thomas could be so lavish and pampering towards his Oxfordshire relations, with his immediate family the reverse was too frequently the case. Presents so freely bestowed in the south were conspicuous by their absence in the north. And in Wigan, also, he was sterner, less gay. Impatient with his children, Thomas unsettled them by his irritability, frightened them with the caustic lash of his tongue. Over-strict, compulsory Bible readings took place on Sundays. Both Joseph and William are said by people who knew them to have been completely lacking in personal opinions. Hardly surprising when Thomas, who had enough for ten men, could not bear to be contradicted! While still very young the boys must have learnt that the better part of a one-sided argument is silence. A perfectionist, their father demanded too much of his children, whom in any case he did not always understand. They were growing up against an alien background. More citified, even affecting a different speech. For unlike Liverpool and other northern towns, Wigan had not received an influx of refugees. Consequently the vowel impurities there were much thicker, and Joseph, who lived longest in the place, had the most pronounced accent.

At approximately the same age that Thomas had been set to work, Joseph was now attending one of the free schools in the vicinity. Contrary to his father he proved a model pupil, retentive of memory, good at English and mathematics. He was also, and as has been indicated by his horoscope, artistic, though this was a bent which least interested Thomas.

6

# CHEMIST'S SHOP

A TOWN to which Thomas returned again and again with his basket and admonitory bottle of worms, was that of St. Helens less than ten miles distant from Wigan. Placed at the southwestern tip of the South Lancashire coalfield its growth was due to coal and its proximity to Liverpool. On the surface it had nothing to recommend it. In the unplanned streets the dingy, red-brick houses had been knocked together with two eyes on haste and none on beauty. On week-days alkali works emitted clouds of acidic smoke which covered the gaunt chimneys, the square church towers, and darkened what remained of the surrounding countryside. And it was abominably smelly. Since water closets were still a novelty, and many homes lacked privies, cesspools abounded. The stench from these, particularly if the sun shone, and the wind was in the wrong direction, could be overpowering.

As has been shown Thomas was no aesthete. How the works ticked, and not the façade was what counted with him, and behind its deplorable exterior St. Helens was exciting and magnificently potential. Since he was shortly to move there, and since it was here that the Beecham fortunes would be coined, a brief history of the town is merited.

Situated in the parish of Prescot, at the junction of the boundaries of the four manors and townships of Windle (in which it stood), Sutton, Eccleston and Parr, its name was derived from

Helena, daughter of merry King Cole of the nursery rhyme. For
centuries a small village had clustered round the chapel of ease
of St. Ellen's, and it was the chapel only which eighteenth-cen-
tury maps showed, the village being considered too unimportant
to be noted. Then, in 1795, something of tremendous significance
occurred. The Sankey Canal, the first in England, was opened
up. Thus Mersey traffic was brought to the district, and with it
numerous other industries, including glass works. So long
delayed, industrialism at first trickled, then rushed ahead. In the
1820s St. Helens was little more than a mining village, orchards
blooming fragrantly in its midst. It was without gas, public
water, a railway, town hall, post office, market building, or
corporate life of its own.

Two decades later all the above amenities existed. Gone was
the rural aspect. Now, anyone wishing to take a quiet country
stroll was obliged to walk through the dwindling fields behind
Westfield Street (a thoroughfare to be extremely important to
the Beechams), to the lanes near Combshop Brow above it, or
further out still to pastoral Denton's Green. Statistics tell their
own story. In 1845 the population of St. Helens as distinct from
the three other townships was 11,800. Fifteen years later this
figure had almost doubled, whilst new buildings continued to
go up at an unprecedented rate.

What of the inhabitants of this boom town which, despite its
startling development had as yet no cocoa rooms, temperance,
clubs, parks, or proper library? The gentry apart, the great
families who had advanced the town, Haddock of coal fame,
Pilkington of glass, and (Sir) David Gamble the manufacturing
chemist, they were a heterogeneous lot. Like Thomas many of
them were country born and bred. Their memories went back
to a rustic St. Helens, and even further, to squalid cabins or
isolated hamlets. Mining, a dangerous job, spawned lusty past-
times. Though the town cockpit had been closed in 1829, colliers
still indulged in bloody pugilistic sports. And when authority
frowned on *these*, there were always the taverns, dance halls,
and brothels to fall back upon. "The people seemed quite ripe
for the Gospel," John Wesley had observed in his journal in 1792
after preaching there. More than fifty years later they were still
ripe, drunkenness being rampant. So, too, were shootings and
assaults, since the miners, the Irish, and the sundry domestic
workers who made up three of the four town groups, were constantly at loggerheads with each other.

It was the colliers, inveterate drinkers and gamblers, who
formed the hard core of the labouring population, and the

inhabitants, cowed by their fiery tempers, gave them a wide berth. A law to themselves, in 1842 when the Mines Regulation Act forbade women to work in mines, they continued to send them, and their children, below ground, it being impossible to clear coal as quickly as it was cut. The practice only stopped when inspectors entered the seams in person to check conditions. But with all their faults the miners were Lancastrians, and so their sins were forgiven them. They especially despised the "foreign" Catholic Irish, who in turn had no truck with the swarthy, dirty, and prolific nailers. In this motley world the glass maker, as did the shepherd of the agricultural one, reigned supreme. Unusually Scottish, he had a pathological love of thrift, was orderly and clean, and kept aloof from all but his own kind.

With so much hot-blooded individualism fermenting, employers despaired of finding a common denominator which would weld the townspeople together. But such vicious birth pangs did not dismay Thomas. A confirmed individualist himself, he was splendidly attuned to the raw atmosphere. Stabilization, as he knew only too well, was a grim battle. It was the growing business possibilities which fascinated him. Years before, when he had left Liverpool, he had actually entertained the idea of settling in St. Helens. But the town had then been undergoing a temporary slump due to the arrival of hordes of starving Irish, and so Wigan had won the day. But perhaps he had made a mistake—always supposing he was capable of making one, of course! Maybe it was here he should have set down his bamboo table, spread out his wares, begun his career?

Meanwhile, time in the town of his election, had passed so quickly that Thomas literally woke one morning to the astonishing realization that he had been there ten years. A whole decade! It was the longest period he had spent in a single place, and by way of celebration he had an enormous handbill printed. On it "Dr. Beecham returned his most grateful thanks to his friends and the public generally for the kind encouragement which he had met with during the last ten years in Wigan and the vicinity, and begged to assure those that 'may favour him with their confidence, that nothing shall be wanting to merit a continuance of the same'. Since it affords an example of the flowery style Thomas then employed in his copy, this bill is worth quoting in greater detail:

"If there be one feeling more than another in the present day," Thomas observed below a caption that TRUTH CONQUERS ALL ASSAILANTS, "it is an earnest desire to find out TRUTH." Some of

his readers would perhaps "have heard tell of the magic properties assigned the river Lethe, in the Mythology of ancient Greece.
In those darker ages superstition held sway, and usurped the
minds of men. Immersion in its water was believed to cause
forgetfulness of past and present woes." But the reader was to
"start not", since "with less Fable, but a far sterner Fact" there
was a Lethe nearer their homes, "whose waters not occasionally,
but at all times flow in one continuous stream of healing benefi-
cence". This was no less than the Laboratory of Nature. "The
remedy grows in every field, it meets us in all our paths, it was
given us by our Great Creator to alleviate the Pains of Disease."
Thomas concluded with a reminder that all his remedies were
composed of Medicinal Herbs, free from any mercurial or other
deleterious substance. "These are not idle words I utter, they are
not the imaginings of a fevered brain, they are stern realities of
long tried practice and unfailing issues. Mr. Envy and Mr. Prejudice, are you prepared to question them?"

This last paragraph is fraught with implications, since it suggests that, despite the kind encouragement he had met there, his
stay in Wigan had not been all beer and skittles. Someone, or
several people, existed who censured his work. Detested snoopers
prowled around, also. Besides medical papers Thomas's "library"
included numerous almanacs and ephemerizes, indispensable to
his fortune telling. "There are many curious things in the world,"
Thomas had pencilled in one of them, "and Man among the lot"
was the most curious indeed! In another, a pryer was advised
to turn to a certain page. If he did so it was to read a distinct
warning to mind his own business. It was possibly to deter busy-
bodies, as much as to jolt forgetful borrowers, if any existed, that
Thomas not only autographed the flyleaves of his books, but
frequently wrote his name across the pages, and in several places
besides. Puns, as well as threats, are revealed, for in another
ephermeris the reader is invited, by a series of conundrums and
heiroglyphics to work out the sum Thomas had paid for it. The
more intelligent might have saved themselves the trouble, however, since the price, 4s. 6d., was clearly indicated in the front.

As yet Thomas was not advertising in newspapers. Handbills
were a preliminary for this. But in the manner of their presen-
tation he doubtless took his cue from advertisers of the day who
were apt to lard their sentences with capitals, and, especially
when puffing medicines, make airy references to truth and a by-
gone age. A man who clung to this style long after it became
old fashioned was James Crossley Eno, of Fruit Salt fame. Eight
years younger than Thomas, he was also intensely individual, an

amateur astrologer, and possessed a crude humour. A booklet he produced on the treatment of the stomach contained advice to the would-be suicide. Interestingly, the Eno Group products were acquired by the firm of Beecham in 1938.

Dipping into his copy of the *Unlearned Alchemist* Thomas may also have been influenced by what he read there. ". . . then do I not fear a good and blessed success in the use of the means which the Lord hath put in my hands for your ease, healing and benefit," the Reverend Richard Mathew wrote of his vegetable pill in 1662. An assertion echoed in Thomas's ". . . it was given to us by our Great Creator to alleviate the Pains of Disease." (The medicinally minded Father evidently had a sympathetic soul. For, "It grieves my heart," he confessed, "as I go up and down the streets, to hear the people cough and wheeze, holding their sides with short breaths when God hath put into my hand so great a blessing for mankind. . . .)

Continued local patronage was now the means of Thomas achieving an ambition which had long been dear to his heart. This was to turn chemist. A shop offered several advantages. It would lessen the need to rush round the countryside so much, a time-wasting process, and also a source of annoyance to Jane. Moreover, since his wife's nerves were chronic, he could keep a firmer eye on the children. The postal business he had been slowly building up could be dealt with more effectively. Most important, it would give him status. For social position Thomas cared nothing, what he desired, what was vital, was professional recognition. As a chemist he could obviously expect far more than that accorded a mere market vendor. Prestige, as it happened, was already on the way, since the following year, 1858, saw his name entered for the first time in Kelly's Directory, as a herbalist. At that period compilers of such works were notoriously snobbish, and Thomas must have established a fair reputation to gain this inclusion. The address given was New Square, but the compilation would have been made the previous year.

Suitable premises were found at 120 Wallgate, the district situated in the centre of Wigan, and which Thomas had given as his address on his original medicine licence. The Beechams were installed there by August of 1857, the little maid, Alice Tickle, apparently accompanying them.

Fitting out the shop was tremendously exhilarating, and Thomas flung himself whole-heartedly into nailing up shelves, fixing drawers, purchasing gilded show jars, drugs, scales and medicines. Since he was to be grocer as well as druggist, stocks of currants and raisins were also bought. Pickles, spices, cigars, black and green teas, coffee canisters, bird seed, scented soaps, drysalters and writing ink. Everything was of the highest quality. A stencil, executed to Thomas's design, was cut, and included the royal coat of arms, though royalty was never known to have made purchases there.

The rhythm of family life was now perceptibly altered. Nomadism temporarily halted, Thomas was home most days, making concoctions and prescriptions, not all of his own device, though at the same time he continued to mix his pills. The children had a permanent father, Jane a full-time husband. She, and Joseph, now ten, took their places behind the counter. Joseph revelled in playing shop-keeper. More than a game, selling could be a ritual. For Jane, however, unable to write, the situation presented difficulties. Illiteracy was, in fact, indirectly to result in a tragedy which occurred a year after the Beechams had transferred to Wallgate.

One Saturday that August a young girl, Elizabeth Smith, entered the shop and requested a pennyworth of laudanum for her father, "very ill with the flux". Jane, who served her, omitted to ask what it was for, to remove the previous label from the bottle, or to mark it appropriately. Back at home Elizabeth's father refused the drastic aid proffered, and the girl's step-mother asked Elizabeth to return the bottle. This she neglected to do, placing it instead in a cupboard. The following Saturday Elizabeth's small brother, Benjamin, felt unwell, and was accidentally dosed with the laudanum, with the consequence that, though an emetic was given, the boy died.

The case was reported in the *Wigan Examiner*, also in the *Pharmaceutical Journal*, then waging a campaign to stop just this kind of evil—the indiscriminate handling of poisons by untrained people. By an ironic coincidence an inquest was held on Friday 13th August, at the Queen's Arms, Newtown. At it Jane stated that she had not put a label on the bottle because Elizabeth Smith frequently called in for laudanum. The coroner, saying that in the present case, Mrs. Beecham's negligence was not the cause of laudanum having been administered to the child, sharply rebuked the custom of giving poisons to children. It was the duty of all chemists personally to supervise their handling. A verdict of accidental death was returned.

Jane had been exonerated. As the coroner had said, whilst the giving of poisons to children was infamous, it was nonetheless widespread, and generally accepted. Nurses of wailing charges often administered gin, sweetened by peppermint, to quiet them. And though composition of several well-known soothing syrups varied between chemists, some narcotic—opium, laudanum, or morphia—was an invariable ingredient of all, one reason why Thomas may have stressed on his handbill that he used no deleterious substances.

The *law* had cleared Thomas's wife. Wigan itself may have been less just. The inquest was held in August 1858. By the end of October the same year Mr. William Pearson the auctioneer was announcing, in the *Observer* and *Examiner* that he had received instructions from the proprietor of No. 120 Wallgate, to sell, by auction, on Monday and Tuesday, 8th and 9th November, the whole of his stock-in-trade and fixtures as Grocer and Druggist, "in consequence of the owner giving up business and leaving the premises".

So *soon?* Thomas had only kept shop fourteen months. He had worked daemonically to this end and spent a great deal of money on the contents as Mr. Pearson made clear in expressing himself "as really anxious that purchasers should inspect the stock before sale, as he confidently believes that a considerable part of it is of such a quality as can only be met with in the finest shops in town". That the auction was to be spread over two days indicated a large number of articles for disposal; that these included 200 lbs. of chemist's soap and a big quantity of ginger, pointed to total flight.

What was behind it? Why the panic haste to leave a place which, on Thomas's own admission, had served him well, and which only a short while back he was thanking for its patronage? Why did Mr. Pearson withhold the name of the proprietor? If Thomas had failed as a chemist, which seems unlikely, or had become bored with a sedentary life, why did he not resume the threads of the old one in Wigan? Perhaps Mr. Envy and Mr. Prejudice were real, and not fictional people. Enemies outnumbered friends, and it only needed Jane's unfortunate slip to set fire to a tinder of criticism.

Thomas was not yet clear of disaster, if indeed it had been disaster which struck. For on 22nd December the beloved little daughter Jane, still only five, died of scarlatina. She was buried two days later, a black Christmas for the disorientated Beechams, who had returned to dingy Hallgate. In the Poors Rate Book for 1859 Thomas's name appears as occupant of a house there, but in the remarks column a Mr. Gannon is mentioned as having paid rates and rental, so his stay must have been extremely brief.

Early in the new year Thomas moved with his family to the

boom town of St. Helens which had so constantly lured his pedlar's feet. At that time it may have seemed a desperate measure. In retrospect it was to prove the wisest decision he ever made.

7

# "THAT SPARK OF WIT"

THE summer was scorching. Europe wilted under aching skies, and in Wigan bottled treacle, beer, and even champagne were consumed by the gallon. Raffish St. Helens needed no excuse to slake its thirst, of course, whilst clothes shops in both towns were besieged for light garments.

For Jane Beecham, approaching a difficult transition in a woman's life, the freak weather cruelly augmented her difficulties. Water was hard to procure, even for cooking. When it did rain the air failed to clear, but pressed down, heavy as lead. Perpetual daymares were the odours arising from hundreds of ashpit privies. The children, the youngest of whom was only four, taxed her energies. And she was servantless. Thomas had rented a cottage in Milk Street cul-de-sac. No. 13, close to the Wesleyan School, the address given on his handbills, was too small for five people, and as usual he appropriated the best room. Matters were not helped, either, by Thomas's apparent immunity to the weather, hardened as he was from childhood to extremes of climate. His chief concern was for his pills. Storage presented serious technical problems. Both light, and atmospheric influences, affected their physical properties, while a high temperature was especially damaging to soft constituents such as soap. Though a good coating materially assisted in keeping the enclosed mass in a proper state of preservation, Thomas eschewed one, instead using a fine liquorice powder. One solution, though hardly profitable, was to make fewer quantities of pills during warm days.

In St. Helens, for the first time, Thomas was imbued with a sense of direction, concentrating exclusively on the manufacture and sale of pills. No longer dissipating talent, professional fortune telling was dropped. So too, were the Royal Toothpowder, the Golden Tincture, the remedy for deafness, and the Female's Friend. The last omission is significant, and may well have been the sharpest thorn in the flesh of Messrs. Envy and Prejudice. Thomas, of course, was by no means alone in marketing a vaguely termed medicine dealing exclusively in women's ailments. Governments of the day were extraordinarily lax in permitting such doubtful remedies. Almost a century was to pass before advertisements of medicines bearing phrases such as "Female's Pills", "Not to be used in cases of pregnancy", and "Never known to fail" were prohibited—implications accidentally, or genuinely, suggesting miscarriage (some of the cures promoted sexual virility, as well as being employed for preventative measures). Left, then, in Thomas's repertoire, was his costive or "herbal" pill, now sold at 6d. a box, and the "magic" cough pill.

Abandoned, also, was the rôle of chemist. His postal business, however, which was large, had followed him, and Thomas relied on this, and selling in the local market.

The return to market trading suggests that the sale of the Wigan equipment, excellent as it was, had not come up to expectations. Thomas was nearly forty, virtually impelled to begin at the bottom again. To a man of lesser calibre this could have spelt disaster. But Beecham possessed more than the courage requisite at this critical juncture of his career. To tenacity and superb self-assurance was allied an ability to rise, phoenix-fashion from dead ashes. He had proved this years before when he had toiled with such seeming fruitlessness with his pedlar's pack in the south. The engraving, on his staff: "Look up! Try again. For where there's 'a will' there's 'a way'," was more than a cliché, it was an article of faith. Never, with all the odds stacked against him, had he once believed he would fail. Another priceless boon was the real enjoyment he derived from selling in the market place. Plunging into the hurly burly of competition there, pitting voice and skill against those of his rivals, personally caught up with the flotsam and jetsam of humanity, this was meat and drink, was life.

St. Helens market was particularly colourful. Since there was no wholesale outlet for farm or garden produce it formed the nucleus to which the countryside came for miles around. A few years before this date heavy congestion had resulted in it being shifted from Church Street to its present position, but it could still be so jammed with people that the surrounding roadway was kept cleared of wheeled traffic from Saturday to Monday. Stalls were heaped with the familiar collection of miscellaneous

E

articles, dilapidated calico wraps, boots, shoes and shawls galore. Fresh and artificial flowers, vegetables, toffee, tripe, fruit, pigs, "crockery by the square yard and old clothes by the cartload". And to keep Thomas on his toes, "stocks of pills of marvellous composition, bottles of infallible remedies for all the ills that flesh was heir to", sparkling and winking under the unflawed summer sky of 1859, or fulgently glowing in the evening naphtha lamps.

Already familiar to a good many customers, Thomas made quick leeway. He had, in any case, always been more acceptable in St. Helens than in Wigan. In a place where Irish, Scotch, and Welsh accents were heard all day long, an Oxfordshire brogue went unremarked. In a town, too, of lusty individualists, eccentricity counted far less than the quality of his goods. Were they better than those of other vendours? Most important, were they worth *buying again*?

Along with the rest of his former stock, Mr. Pearson had evidently disposed of the bamboo table, since Thomas now used a fish barrel, whilst part of a door served as a tray which held his wares. On wet days he still sheltered under his enormous umbrella. As always his energy was fantastic. "He deserved all he got," a contemporary recalled. "No-one worked harder, or stuck to it more than he did. And what he had not sold by the end of the evening he gave away." Pills were also available at his Milk Street home, people knocking on the door and purchasing them by the pennyworth.

Back in the market rough and tumble, living in the infinitely more conducive atmosphere of a raw, as opposed to a settled, town, Thomas's spirits quickly revived. Hurt and humiliation faded away. Even the grief caused by the loss of the little daughter became rapidly healed. Thomas was a past master in believing what he wanted to, however much evidence might contradict fact. Easy to tell himself he had intended settling in St. Helens— eventually. It was part of a progressive plan. Wigan had been a testing place, a springboard for ambition, no more. And before long, another interest, engrossing him, helped to erase the memory of recent setbacks. This was his initiation into advertising.

Hitherto Thomas had fought shy of a medium which had seemed an unnecessary expense. At first restricted to Wigan and the vicinity, later successfully conducted by post and in his shop, business had been adequate. But now it was obvious that it could be possible to be too cautious with money. If he was to consolidate his modest reputation in St. Helens, extend sales to towns sheer time made it difficult to travel to, then his name must be kept constantly before the public. A public growing increasingly literate, although compulsory school attendance was still more than twenty years away.

Another previous deterrent may well have been the high cost of newspapers which most of his customers could not have afforded. Many of them were as much as fivepence, and in some towns, including St. Helens, the inhabitants clubbed together to read papers communally in rooms and taverns.

The inhibiting price was a result of the war which had been going on between the newspaper world and the government as far back as 1712, when authority, determined to curb the activities of the Press, imposed a punitive stamp duty, and advertisement tax. The latter was not lifted till 1853, the same year, as it happened, when St. Helens, discarding its picturesque town crier, came to have its own newspaper. With the abolition of the stamp duty in 1855 there remained only an irritating "tax on knowledge", to be repealed in 1861. Their wings freed, newspaper proprietors could afford to print more cheaply, the public to buy their papers in greater quantities. Figures spoke for themselves. In 1853 some 640 newspapers were in circulation in Great Britain. By the end of the century the number had increased to more than 3,000.

An avid newspaper reader, Thomas may also have been inspired at this period by the example of two other patent medicine vendors, James Morison, and "Professor" Thomas Holloway. Both men had advertised consistently for years. Both were rich, and far too astute to waste profits. If Thomas knew their histories he must have been still more impressed.

Morison (who had died in 1840, in the act, it was said, of reaching for his own medicine, and who had shrewd successors), was a Scotsman. For thirty-five years he had endured "inexpressible suffering" before discovering the remedy which allayed his pains, and those of thousands of others. This was a vegetable pill swallowed at bed-time with a glass of lemonade. He had lived stylishly in Hamilton Place, London, and in the decade before his death paid the government no less a sum than £60,000 in stamp duties. His ingenious advertising had drawn growls from Carlyle. Men and women, the historian complained, fancied their religion should be a kind of Morison's Pill, which they had only to swallow once, and all would be well.

More eventful, Holloway's life story curiously resembled Beecham's in certain details.

A soldier's son from Devonport, Holloway had started out as a street fakir. By means of a little tin box set up on a wooden tripod he retailed his drugs at a penny a box in one of the more squalid quarters of London. While still selling in this fashion he helped an Italian leech vendor obtain a hospital testimonial to popularise his medicine, which he subsequently pinched for himself, and followed up with a brand of pills. Both he, and the cheated Italian, drifted into the debtor's prison. What happened to the leech vendor is not known, but four years after regaining his freedom, Holloway found himself on the royal road to success. Long before Thomas, he became the most important advertiser in the country. In 1842 he was spending £5,000 a year on this medium. Splendid offices were opened up in the Strand, and eight years later advertising expenditure had leapt to an annual £20,000.

Thomas's first advertisement appeared in the *St. Helens Intelligencer* on 6th August, 1859. This newspaper, which had made its bow under the more basic title of *What's Wanted*, cost three-halfpence, and besides the townships of Windle, Eccleston, Sutton and Parr, covered seven districts, including Widnes, Preston and Appleton. It thus reached a large public. Printed on the front page, readers, below the challenging slogan, WORTH A GUINEA A BOX, were informed that: "One trial will convince you that BEECHAM'S PILLS are the best in the world for bilious and nervous disorders, wind and pain of the stomach, headache, giddiness, fullness and swelling after meals, drowsiness, cold chills, loss of appetite, shortness of breath, etc., etc."

A testimonial from a Mr. Mason, Boot and Shoe Maker of Golborne, followed:

Sir:
About five years ago my wife became afflicted with that distressing complaint, wind and pain at the stomach, and through the violent attack of spasms she was reduced so low in strength as not likely to recover. She tried a many things, but all failed to do her good, but to our great joy one box of your pills perfectly cured her.

These pills were sold wholesale and retail by the proprietor, who would send one box post free for eight stamps to any address.

Apart from the novelty of it being Thomas's first advertisement, this copy is interesting for several other reasons.

He remained an erratic speller all his life, and if there were any mistakes the printer had ironed them out. In contrast to the dramatic references to Truth and the river Lethe in his Wigan handout, the tone is commendably restrained. Indeed, far more lurid were Holloway's claims immediately above it. His ointment "went to the very core of all diseases which afflict the body. It disappears under the friction of the hand, as if it were literally drawn inwards by some internal force", curing, amongst much else, open sores, hard tumours, abscesses, cancers, old wounds, in fact, every "species of inflammation and suppuration".

The advertisement is also unique in that it deviates in two particulars from the classical puffing of this kind of product then in use. There is no reference to the discovery of the medicine; no clincher from a patron or celebrity. And on both counts Thomas never wavered. Only when elderly did he allude to his findings at the Lawn Farm, and then to journalists, not prospective buyers. Whilst his appeal, although he liked to boast that aristocracy swallowed his pills—"I have positive proof of it!"—was, first and foremost, to the poor people. "To those who do not care to apply for medicine to public institutions and do not want a doctor for treating slight ailments."

But the salient point of the advertisement, of course, is that the famous slogan is adopted right from the start. In this Thomas was again well ahead of his time, since slogans were not fashionable for at least another ten years.

As with the pill formula all kinds of legends were to spring up regarding the origin of the phrase. In those days a guinea was the virtual fee for a confinement. In his History of St. Helens Brockbank states that a Mrs. Ellen Butler, "a lady of good family and business aptitude", became a purchaser of Mr. Beecham's Pills. So enthusiastic did she wax over their virtues that she liked to declare to anyone listening that they were worth a guinea a box, "thus crystallising a phrase that has since become familiar wherever the English language is spoken".

It has always been accepted in the family that the saying was inspired by a woman in St. Helens market place who approached Thomas and demanded another box. "They're worth a guinea to me, lad." Thomas, himself, sometimes referred to this incident. However, in old age he was occasionally given to flat contradiction, and in 1897 when replying to a query from the editor of the Chemist and Druggist he stated categorically that he himself, and no other, had struck out from the mental anvil that "spark of wit which had made the pills a household word in every quarter of the globe".

Whatever the origin of the slogan the globe had yet to be conquered. Meanwhile, Thomas's advertisement, complete with its lucky spark of wit, continued to grace the pages of the Intelligencer, unaltered, for the remainder of the year. Each time it appeared Thomas checked it against the original copy, carefully filed away. And so the months ground on, December proving as icy as the summer had been hot. Frost was unparalleled for its severity. In London 20,000 people skated in Regents Park. In St. Helens all outdoor work was temporarily suspended. Despite this the *Wigan Observer* remarked early in January that trade in the lively Merseyside town had never been in a more satisfactory condition. In glassmaking, chemical manufacture, iron foundries, and potteries, the inhabitants were kept fully occupied. Colliery proprietors were particularly pleased.

Not more so than Thomas who, with business ticking over nicely in Milk Street, was well satisfied with his change of address. 1859 which he begun so bleakly, had ended on a distinct note of hope. The walls of the Beechams' tiny cottage were becoming increasingly defaced with sales records.

8

# THE BREAK WITH JANE

WELL before the turn of the century Thomas was to be the largest advertiser in the United Kingdom. Such seasoned veterans as Holloway and Morison's successors would be left far behind in the field. Yet it is strange that, having tackled the medium so late, he should still, for a few more years, continue to move in it with all the caution of a cat treading water. Not easily was he convinced that publicity, at least on a wide scale, was essential to business. Adequate returns and hard figures must relentlessly hammer home their points. He had a great deal of the peasant in him, and inherited prudence was never more evinced. "I'm not going to lay out a sovereign unless I can get a guinea back," became a favourite axion.

Throughout 1860 he contented himself by advertising locally only, transferring to the *St. Helens Weekly News* when this paper made its début in September. Two years later the title was changed to the *St. Helens Newspaper and Advertiser*. Thomas retained his original copy, merely adding a fresh testimonial from a customer at Pendlebury, the last sentence of which read:

"As the newspapers say they (the pills) are worth a guinea a box. I declare they are worth five guineas a box," evidence that the slogan was capturing popular imagination.

On the whole 1860 was a plodding, uneventful year, with Thomas busy each day of the week consolidating gains, energetically promoting new sales. A curious phenomenon occurred on 15th September, as bad luck would have it, Saturday market day. The town sky became overshadowed during the day by millions of gnats. Especially active in the market place, and thick as clouds, they flew around till evening, when, with the abruptness of a horde of locusts, they vanished. The incident was never explained, though the more superstitious declared it was an ill omen. As it happened the Prince Consort died in December, whilst that winter St. Helens suffered a mild slump. Soup kitchens were opened up, and a Wigan reporter, gloomily contradicting January optimism, observed that "trade is bad here, the people have little money to spare". Fortunately, however, the recession proved brief, and economic prosperity was quickly restored.

In the new year Thomas, pressing his wholesale and retail trade, decided to revise his prices, and by doing so bring them into line with the larger proprietors of patent medicines. The altered charges, which took effect on and after 1st January, 1861, were set out on handbills, printed and handwritten, and which, since he cherished the milestones of his career, he carefully preserved. The pills now came in three boxes:

| | | | | |
|---|---|---|---|---|
| 9½d. | ...... | ...... | 6s. 6d. | per dozen |
| 1s. 3½d. | ...... | ...... | 10s. | ,, ,, |
| 2s. 9d. | ...... | ...... | 25s. | ,, ,, |

A 15 per cent discount for cash with orders, or on receipt of goods was to be allowed, and at three months accounts would be net. The whole of the carriage was to be paid by the consignee, Thomas refusing to take the responsibility for any loss, or pilfering from the parcels occurring during transit. These terms were to be strictly enforced (several of which, as will be shown, were to become sore points with retailers), whilst in no case whatsoever was the full discount to be permitted except for prompt cash. Scrupulously honest himself, with a horror of debts, Thomas imposed his own high standards on his purchasers.

At this time his sole help, apart from casual market labour, was his son Joseph. The boy was badgered into constant service, his leisure completely monopolized. Writing out addresses, gumming labels on to boxes, packaging, even being initiated into the ritual of mixing, Joseph often had to rise early, before school, to fulfil his manifold tasks. Not yet thirteen, soon like the liniment advertisements where every picture told a story, his red eyes and excessive pallor, came to the attention of his headmaster. So severely was Thomas reprimanded that chores were, for a space, relaxed. However, it is doubtful if the father ever drove the son harder than he drove himself. Joseph had inherited both a passion for work, and a natural fascination for pill-making. Every aspect of it intrigued him.

The child was now attending Moorflat School, an Anglican establishment housed in a dingy building in Baldwin Street. Initially for the "sons of respectable tradesmen", a higher education was offered there than at other free schools in the town. An impressive curriculum included euclid, algebra, mechanics, book-keeping with double entry, mensuration, drawing, painting and chemistry. Joseph continued to be a model pupil, mathematics easily his best subject. Later, it was said of him that he could add up long columns of figures four and five deep with greater facility than most people could one. For a moderate fee music was taught, together with the use of the harmonium. The fee seems to have been found, for in only a few years time Joseph was playing the harmonium in a local church. All his life the organ remained his favourite instrument, while, after work, music was to be his great love.

With his brother and sister, Joseph went to Sunday school at Ormskirk Street Church, Thomas having defected to Congregationalism almost immediately on settling in the town. The Beecham parents sat in a plain, uncushioned pew. In due course Thomas is thought to have been a lay preacher, and though not on the Lancashire Congregational Union's official list as such, may well have been an intermittent one. Gone was the dandyism of his earlier days, either pressure of work, or his strained relations with his wife, making him now indifferent to appearance. An amusing incident illustrating just how trampish he could look, occurred about this date. An appeal for subscriptions was made in church. Several affluent members volunteered moderate sums. Then suddenly "a small man in an untidy frock coat" sprang to his feet and boomed out his donation. A hundred pounds! Gasps, followed by doubtful stares. The benefactor did not look as if he could clap two pennies together, let alone pounds. But Thomas made good his offer. Since he liked to keep silent about his philanthropies this was a rare occasion when one was publicly announced.

For holidays Jane Beecham occasionally took the children on day trips to Southport. But her health was worsening all the time, and she had now become subject to frequent hallucinations. Often she would hear the children cry out at night, when in fact they were fast asleep. Though Thomas claimed that his pill healed nervousness and general debility, and though at least one of his customers had written to say three doses had completely cured him "of frightful dreams and strange imaginations", for the proprietor's wife there was no alleviation. In an effort to allay her symptoms Jane was now spending more and more time in the taverns. A vicious circle, heavy drinking only increasing her vagaries.

It was, therefore, to Aunt Jane, Thomas's second youngest sister, that the three little Beechams were usually packed off in the school holidays. A month after Thomas himself, this Aunt Jane had married the farmer for whom she kept house in Hogshaw, Buckinghamshire, the tiny village next door to Granborough, knowledge of which Thomas was to deny to the editor of Tit-Bits. Her husband, William Butcher Hughes, was a well-to-do farmer, and as such he and his family looked down on Jane's labouring kinsfolk. Nevertheless, Jane saw a great deal of her own relatives. Amply proportioned, and though possessing her family's snappy temper, she was adored in her own, being warm-hearted, motherly, and religious.

The Hughes' farm was fine and roomy, and visits there were eagerly anticipated. The days stretched long as years, with everything geared to enjoyment. Crisp country air, instead of foul chemical odours, expanded the lungs of the northern niece and nephews, who ran wild with their numerous cousins. Play would be pleasingly interspersed with treks to other aunts, and to Granny Morris at Curbridge. So much chaos, and simple hospitality, was in sharp contrast to the Milk Street life, where voices, because of the pace of work, had to be kept muted. Where there was no social whirl, no entertaining, and where Thomas's caustic tongue, Jane Beecham's nervy behaviour, too often douched youthful spirits.

Joseph, especially, gained from these occasions. His sallow cheeks filled out, whilst the physical lethargy induced by over-work miraculously disappeared. He liked the country as his father, brought up in it, had welcomed the change of the indus-trial towns. The huge skies, the dense hedges with their seasonal bursts of blackberries and willow herbs. The dimensions of the house, enormous after a tiny cottage; and, in due course, and particularly, the company of one cousin, Sarah Ann Hughes. . . . There was teasing, in the boisterous fun. His accent, so much cruder than his brother, or sister's, provoked banter. But he could defend himself by mimicking the slower Oxfordshire speech in a way he would not have dared do had Thomas, who spoke, it, been present.

To the Hughes, with their extrovert bunch of youngsters, the St. Helens trio presented curious studies in inhibition. Joseph shy, reticent, only relaxing as the holidays drew to a close. Sarah, dreamy, not very bright, and William with his own brand of seriousness, already an embryo pedant. Thomas repaid his sister's kindness with innumerable presents, sometimes out of all proportion to services rendered. Once it was a hundred pounds, on another occasion he gave her a valuable ring. Suddenly, and much too soon, he would be amongst his children again, rushing down from Lancashire, or wherever he happened to be on business. A final supper at the Merry Horn, last farewells, and friendly Buckinghamshire was left behind. Back in St. Helens the town would seem twice as dirty, three times smellier, whilst their father, who, for a brief interval, had been a gay, cheerful human being, was now changed back into a pill-making machine, occupied from dawn to dusk, irritable, snorting dire threats at them if they so much as breathed. Pills, pills, pills, they dominated existence! They were not so much a means to an end as the end itself.

Dominating the children's days, too, was the lengthening shadow cast by their parents' incompatability. In the autumn of 1861 it exploded into public limelight when, at the petty sessions, Thomas charged an ostler, Samuel Gordon, with using threatening language, and his wife, Jane, with beating him. Ironically backfiring, the case also touched on, though it failed to reveal, Thomas's reason for leaving Wigan.

According to the *Weekly News* which reported the proceedings on 14th September, "Dr. Beecham", as he still styled himself, had returned home from the market at 11 p.m. Though there seemed some doubt, he appeared to have been drinking with a neighbour, Mrs. Lowe, in Milk Street. To his annoyance he found himself locked out of his house. Squatting on the window sill he tried to wake Joseph to let him in. But it was Jane who appeared on the scene instead. She noisily harangued him, whereupon, and on his own admission, he threw her into the street. Jane had been drinking herself, for she fell back, "her head being heavier than the rest of her body". It was at this point that Gordon came up and abused Thomas.

The bench, which included a member of the famous Pilkington family, appeared to be more conversant with Thomas's activities than those of a single rowdy evening, for he was pressed into giving his reasons for leaving Wigan. At first reluctant to answer, but goaded by repeated questioning, Thomas muttered at last that it had been to better himself. Both he and Gordon were bound over to keep the peace. For a few years longer the unhappy state of affairs continued between husband wife when, prudently, they decided to separate, and Jane went off to live in a different part of the town. Joseph joined her. The two remaining children stayed with their father, or lodged with relatives.

By now Thomas's advertising was extended to include the *Cambridge Independent Press*, and the *Wigan Observer*. Chemists sold his pills in Wigan, and also a Mr. Thomas Wall, of the *Observer* office—evidently a man of parts, for he also sold musical instruments. In addition to his new prices Thomas was offering to send boxes post free for eleven, or thirty-six stamps. He also proudly claimed that his pills were retailed by every druggist in the kingdom. Exaggerated as it sounds at this date, Thomas *did* have wholesale agents at Bow Church Yard, London, and Sydney Street, Cambridge. A piece of business chicanery was that he had "at great expense" obtained a patent for his pills, a picture of the patent stamp appearing in some of his advertisements. In fact, Thomas never patented them, since this would have necessitated divulging the ingredients. But, like the royal coat of arms on his Wigan stencil, it was doubtless designed to impress customers, though the "great expense" could not have fooled the knowledgeable, since the price for a three year period was approximately only £25.

For the next decade or so, and piecemeal, like a surveyor inching out his tape measure, Thomas increased his advertising, reaching out to county after county, until at last he covered the whole country. Twenty per cent return, he reiterated, was what he expected from it. Advertisements were inserted in a paper for a year, paid for in advance, Thomas promising to renew the following one if satisfied. Usually, however, he advertised for a three-year period in the same newspaper, by the end of which time he declared he knew if it was worth while continuing to do so or not.

Still writing his own copy he varied this only minutely, changing the wording here and there, adding and subtracting testimonials. He did not startle, and there were no innovations. There were none anywhere, for the golden age of advertising had yet to dawn. As had once been the case with Thomas, most manufacturers needed solid convincing that advertising was

necessary. Was it not really rather *vulgar*? Bracketing respectable commodities with salves and trusses could surely only scare
the public, not attract it? Word of mouth had always been a
sound enough method, while, if distant markets were wanted,
travellers abounded who could take the goods on the road.

Even more distrustful of advertising than die-hard business
men were the actual newspaper editors. Although abolition of
the taxes on knowledge had enabled them to sell their papers
cheaper, pride forbade them to admit that it was the advertiser
who substantially aided them to publish at a penny. Thus the
rules were many, and prohibiting. Pictures were virtually dis-
allowed. Also ruled out was big black type. By common consent
newspapers banned the use of any type larger than minion. In
an effort to defeat this restriction advertisers would repeat the
firm's name for hundreds of lines, relying on the sheer weight
of a cumulative effect. One paper, *The Times*, hitting back at this
escape device, insisted that each line should be punctuated with
explanatory matter. Thomas, himself, was not above employing
the trick, though on the whole he refrained. Whilst temporarily
it outwitted editors, it also tended to make enemies of them.
Much worse, it made copy-writing, which was interesting,
dull.

Business continued to flourish. So much so that by the
autumn of 1863 Thomas was able to move to more suitable
premises. The transfer, heralded by the caption FLITTED, which
many of the townspeople could appreciate only too well, was
announced in the *St. Helens Newspaper*. "Mr. Beecham, the
Proprietor of the World Renowned Pills begs to inform the
public of St. Helens that he has moved from Milk Street to 32
Westfield Street, where a box of the Finest Medicine in the
World can be had for 9½d."

The new cottage, whose rateable value stood at £10 4s. od.
and was owned by a Mr. Fishwick, was not much larger than
the old one, being only three up and down, but its position was
priceless, since Westfield Street had become a thriving thoroughfare. Opening at one end into busy Church Street, where were
the post office and the Fleece Hotel at which all the important
visitors stayed, at the other it forked off to Boundary Hill, and
Cropper's Hill, colloquially dubbed Combshop Brow, in memory
of the trade which had once existed there. And along both these
streamed inhabitants from neighbouring villages.

At last discarding the living-room Thomas now made up his
pills in a backyard shed. Townspeople still bought pennyworths
at a time. Never allowed into the house, they were obliged to

knock on an especially contrived window. A glass panel would be slid open, the sale effected, then the pane hurriedly closed again. With his hatred of priers Thomas was possibly wise to the local saying that "everyone in St. Helens was related", and was not taking any chances.

Change was an unfailing tonic. Re-galvanized, pills were pounded and mixed in such quantities that an aroma, as distinctive as the town's prevailing chemical smells, came to hang over the cottage. So curative was this held to be that people stood outside, deliberately sniffing, and swearing that they were healed merely by inhaling the vapours. The scope of Thomas's manufacture is illustrated by the anecdote of the traveller in drugs who called on a nearby chemist. Told no order was required that day he was advised, instead, to "try the chap down the road who makes a few pills". Off he hurried, only to be back very quickly, wryly protesting: "That fellow you sent me to is out of his mind. He asked for *three tons* of aloes!"

Dealings with wholesale houses, ingredients ordered by the ton, leading druggists in key cities retailing his pills, necessitated a far more advanced method of production than that of pestle, mortar, and pill board. Very little machinery being available at that period, Thomas, inventive and adaptable, made much of his own, improving on his creations as time went by, and exigencies arose. Manual effort was replaced by steam power, this in its turn, and by the natural process of evolution, being finally superseded by electricity.

In 1864 Thomas added to his status by enrolling as a member of the United Society of Chemists and Druggists. This society had been founded some three years previously for the express purpose of giving chemists and druggists in the United Kingdom a representative organisation. It also advocated an education test to safeguard the interests of those in business. Both it, and its rival, the Pharmaceutical Society, were responsible for the Pharmacy Act receiving royal assent four years later. A provision of this Act was that requiring that all those who desired to commence in business as pharmaceutical chemists, or chemists and druggists, to dispense prescriptions containing poisons, should pass a qualifying examination. Long overdue, this measure was motivated to make the kind of accident which had occurred to little Benjamin Smith in Wigan, impossible. With the passing of the Act, the chief reasons for the existence of the United Society of Chemists and Druggists, were realized. And when, in 1875 its initiator, a Mr. Wade, went over to the "enemy camp" of the

Pharmaceutical Society, it petered into oblivion. Nevertheless, joining it was a personal triumph for Thomas. Immensely proud of the certificate, a resplendent affair executed in gold, and gay colours, it hung on a wall of his home where the over-curious, craning their necks through the pennyworth window, might see it, and be suitably impressed.

It was also now that Thomas dropped his "Doctor" title, a misnomer the Society would not have countenanced for a moment. The law itself remained more lenient. Not until 1944 was the use of "Dr." forbidden on the name of a marketed product.

Plain Mr. Beecham, doing so well, was badly in need of regular help. When he was fifteen, or slightly earlier, Joseph finished school, and officially joined his father in the business. Unofficially, of course, he had been Thomas's left hand for several years, and knew the Z to A of pill-making.

9

# MOUNTING FORTUNE

B E E C H A M advertisements now carried cautionary reminders to the effect that unless the name and address of the product was on the government stamp affixed to each box of pills they were a forgery. Imitation, a back-handed form of compliment, was to plague the firm for many years.

By 1865 Thomas had added wholesale agents at Liverpool and Manchester to his list. The following year it was augmented by three more, at Wolverhampton, Leeds, and York. Accounts, of course, could not continue to be scrawled haphazardly on cottage walls, and were kept in a dark green book with a red binding. Extremely neat, into the remarks column went the discounts allowed for cash orders, whether the pills were dispatched in part payment for advertising, whilst warning red ink recorded the rare defaulter. The latter was given a second chance then, if debts remained unhonoured, business was permanently severed.

This order book, stretching between 1865 and 1874 makes

startling reading. After the long, hard years of painful slogging it is abundantly clear that a concrete break-through had been achieved. From now on it was to be victory all the way. From start to finish there is no check, no slowing down of mounting fortune. Year after year the astonishing gross amounts leap up: £2,532 19s. 5d. in 1865, £3,510 18s. in 1866, and by 1867 £4,556 0s. 10d.! Customers, at the start, ranged as far afield as York, Exeter, and Dumfries, substantiating Thomas's boast that his pills could be obtained at every druggist in the country. Confidence in his methods and products alike is indicated by the fact that large firms such as Raines of Liverpool, and Sanger of London who were placing monthly orders in 1865, were still placing them in 1874, and in ever increasing quantities.

A curious aspect about the orders is how, with almost unvarying consistency, they rise sharply in January and July every year, but drop notably each June and December. Presumably, following the Christmas rush, and with winter ailments in mind, firms stocked up for the new year. Less easily explained are the July demands, though in meeting them Thomas must, in the main, have overcome the technical difficulty of preserving his wares in warm weather.

£4,556 0s. 10d. . . . . fantastic as this sum is, it would prove mere chicken feed by the time the last entry had been scratched into the green book. Nonetheless it was a handsome income for a man whose only help at this period, other than market labour, was the youthful Joseph. How had it been achieved? The answer must lie in Thomas's total dedication to work. He never took holidays, and apart from occasional threatre-going, had no hobbies. Overheads were nominal, and he even kept his one, full-time assistant short of cash. Years later, acknowledging applause for his rôle as impresario at the Theatre Royal, Drury Lane, Joseph confessed to "paying a shilling, at a time when shillings were none too plentiful", to listen to opera in the gallery.

Thomas worked some fourteen hours a day. Joseph, though he was to improve on this, still found time to play. He was growing into a socially-minded young man. When the unplentiful shillings permitted he attended concerts in Liverpool. Every Tuesday he played the harmonium at services held in Groves School. Organ playing at two other churches was to follow. He became an enthusiastic member of the town cricket club, and in 1876 was co-founder of the St. Helens cycling club.

On the surface it seems paradoxical that it should have been the extrovert father who spurned society, whilst the retiring,

semi-articulate son, to whom new faces could be a refined tor-
ture, it was who flung himself whole-heartedly into group activities. But the riddle is partly explained by the fact that St. Helens
itself was undergoing a striking metamorphosis. Almost gone was
its raucous, boom town atmosphere. An art gallery, proper library
and park were still in the future, and it would be a long while
yet before, as a local vicar deplored, Englishmen here ceased to
give the impression they were "anything but a suction machine".
The place was being tidied up, however, pummelled and moulded
into a workable unity. The intrinsic individualism of its inhabitants, once the despair of employers, had become its saving
grace. Country past-times, such as pigeon flying and foot-racing,
were fast replacing the old prize fights. Logical sequences were
sports clubs. Whole generations were springing up, too, who
only remembered town life, and having no quarrels with immigrants glanced tolerantly at their neighbours. Catholic and
Protestant were intermarrying, even the colliers, their tempers
tamed, were beginning to fraternize. Inevitably Thomas, the lone
ranger, was part of the old order, whilst Joseph, sober, conven-
tional, ambitious, and quiet, was sliding into the new pattern
with tailor-made precision.

Some of the spectacular returns were being invested in
property.
By 1866 Thomas was the owner/occupier of 29 Westfield
Street. Since this street came to be renumbered, it may have been
the former No. 32, but the rateable value was slightly higher,
£12 15s. and the premises were described as a cottage/workshop.
He also owned No. 27, at that time inhabited by another tenant.
In 1873 Thomas occupied both 27 and 29 Westfield Street, the
latter cottage apparently being his place of manufacture.
Financial security had made it possible for William, unlike
his brother, Joseph, to be privately educated. Though pill making
bored him, he had a vague leaning towards medicine, eventually
studying at University College, Liverpool, and later enrolling as
a medical student in a London Hospital. Without Joseph's drive
or brilliance, he shared his enthusiasm for sports, particularly
cycling, when bicycles came to be manufactured in quantity in
the 1870s. William's sole claim to fame was to come third in a
championship contest. Cycling from Sankey Bridge near Warrington, to the Bird I' Hand, St. Helens, via Rainhill and Prescot,
he covered the four miles in the then commendable time of
49 minutes 11 seconds. This was in 1877. Things were happening
fast in the Beechams' personal lives, as in their careers, so

'Bilious Iago'—an advertisement from the mid-nineties

Oh, Mr Porter

What the wild waves said

that well before this date three marriages would have taken place.

The first was on 29th April, 1871, at the Anglican church of St. Thomas's, Eccleston, of Thomas's daughter, Sarah Ann, then almost twenty-one. Her husband, Edward Absom Pemberton, who was the same age, was a joiner, and his father belonged to the cream of the working class, being a glass maker. Though Thomas entertained doubts about Edward, who was, indeed, to desert his wife, he raised no solid objections to the union. Thomas's profession in the register is given as that of chemist, a definition he now adhered to, though hitherto he had styled himself botanist and herbalist. Sarah's was a rather simple mentality, and the young woman's face which gazes somewhat vacuously out of a photograph taken around this time reveals a markedly low forehead. Suffering fools ungladly, Thomas patronized her, and no doubt she was as relieved to leave home as he was to have a not very interesting daughter off his hands. The Edward Pembertons had one son, Edward, who later became clerk in the business. Musical, he never really found his vocation.

The two other marriages referred to will be dealt with in the next chapter.

Despite pressure of manufacture, Thomas was still an indefatigable traveller. To be sedentary for any length of time irked him excruciatingly. Besides, he liked to call personally on chemists and wholesale houses with whom he dealt. In this way a large number of friendships were formed, though acquaintances were seldom, if ever, brought home. He also delighted in keeping in touch with past cronies, particularly those he had known in the south in his shepherding days. And it is because of this habit that the only personal letter to come to light was written.

One day in January 1872, he happened to be in Banbury on business. Whilst there he saw a Cropredy carrier, the rickety, covered waggons which took parcels and passengers into town, rolling along the street. Suddenly, unexpectedly, he was struck by a wave of acute nostalgia. Not for his early struggles, since he was never to be guilty of gilding hardship, but for old associations. For, at fifty-one, the cocky adolescent he had once been, and for the kindly, homely people who, like himself, had been poor, but always cheerful and good company. Rushing across to the cart he plied the driver with questions, which the latter answered as best he could. Back in St. Helens a few weeks later, Thomas, memories still churning inside him, penned a letter to a Mr. Thomas Giles, in Australia. Giles, it may be recalled, had worked under him as a boy at the Lawn Farm, and his family

F

had been especially hospitable to Mr. Chamberlin's gifted shepherd, This letter is quoted in full:

FROM: T. BEECHAM PATENTEE      ST. HELENS,
AND PROPRIETOR                 LANCASHIRE.
OF BEECHAM'S PILLS             February 12th, 1872

Respected Friend Mr. Thomas Giles
formerly of Cropredy, N. Banbury.

Many years have gone past since you and I was at Cropredy Lawn together, and I am sure you never expected to see or hear from me again.

Hundreds of times have I wondered where you was, and what you was doing, and about three or four years since I called at Cropredy to see if I could see or hear anything of you and Joseph Hazlewood, who used to help me at The Lawn, but I found Joseph was somewhere in Birmingham, and no one could tell me where you was. Thus time passed on, till about the 20th of last month as I was in Banbury upon business, and the first thing I noticed was a Cropredy Carrier. I asked him if any of your family was living at Cropredy—the answer was no—but your sister was living in Banbury he said, and told me where, so for the first time since I was at The Lawn, I that day had the pleasure to see Hannah.

She knew me in a moment although I had no knowledge of her, she looked jolly and well, and very much increased in bulk since I saw her thirty years ago. She showed me a photograph of a Family, in a farmyard, which she said was you and your family and also your own homestead.

I was happy to hear you was doing well and that you turned your talent to a better account than being satisfied in a most miserable condition, such as all are placed in who work their lives out on a farm for a paltry few shillings a week. As you have worked yourself out of such an hopeless gulf I trust you are able to look back with pleasure upon the past and able to recognise the Unseen-Hand which has brought you thus far on the journey of life, and the voice which has often said—

My Presence shall go with thee,
and I will give thee rest!

That voice, my Dear Friend, is if you will but heed it, the best and richest companion in our life's journey.

Now as regards business, by what Hannah told me you are doing well and with respect to myself I would not change with any man living.

I suppose you never need any Physic, well if you don't it is all the better. If you do just try my pills which I send you enclosed—one bottle of each sort.

If you could just step into my workshop at the end of a day when we are making, you would wonder who in the world was going to take them all. I often make over one hundredweight in one day. I have the best machinery of anyone known (all works by steam power) the most effective part of it is my own construction. My sale extends to every town in England, Wales, Scotland, and to some parts of Australia (but the wholesale houses whom I supply send them there) and I send now many to Africa.

I send by this post six of my newspapers for your perusal, perhaps you may find something in them to amuse you, if it does not instruct you. The chasm between you and I is a wide one, therefore I expect English news does not reach you often.

In conclusion I beg to tender you and your family also my kindliest respects and best wishes, and trust that health and prosperity will not forsake you, and while you employ those blessings don't forget the fact that the time will come when they most prove a blessing or a curse, but use your time and talent in such a way that when the last sands of the hourglass of life becomes united to the Angel of Death you may then hear that still small voice say "Well Done".

From yours very Respectfully,<br>THOMAS BEECHAM.

Such colourful writing makes it all the more regrettable that it has been impossible to find any other personal correspondence. Yet if this *had* been traced, and only a single letter was to be selected for publication, it would be difficult to imagine a more rewarding one than the above. For here is everything about the man. Thomas's loathing for the farm rut, undiminished by time, or good fortune. Physically he had remained unaltered, being immediately recognizable to Hannah. Paternal instinct, so strong outside his own family, is well indicated in the fourth paragraph. The labourer protégé (Giles was several years Thomas's junior) had made good, had achieved that most desirable of states, independence—subsequent research has revealed that Giles was a property owner. Stressed, too, is the strong, uncomplicated religious creed. Always, but always, the Unseen-Hand favoured the user of talents. As inevitable as day following night. The latent poet is also well to the fore. An unliterary man would have written: "Time went by", instead of, "Thus time passed on". While, "I had that day the pleasure to see Hannah", would probably have ground out a banal "I saw Hannah again".

And last, but not least, burns the canny business instinct. Working with him on the farm, Giles must have seen Thomas making his pill. He would, perhaps, have remembered the basic ingredients. If so, it was Thomas's achievements, rather than his products, which would impress. And so the work, and not the physic, is emphasized. But, just in case Giles *had* forgotten, a bottle of each medicine is dispatched, together with newspapers no doubt including Thomas's advertisements. These, at least, would evince admiration, be passed round the family circle, shown to neighbours, and so an infinitesimal boost be given the important market Thomas was just beginning to tap.

This letter was to have a curious history. Fondly preserved in the Giles household, it was extracted from a drawer by a male descendant while its possessor lay dying in the same room. The new owner tried unsuccessfully to sell it commercially. Then, into his village in New South Wales, there came a travelling showman. On an impulsive mood the letter was handed to this man, to be added to the latter's "museum" of relics and antiquities. Subsequently the act was regretted, but all attempts to find the showman again ended in a blank. He had pushed off into the outback.

Like Thomas, Giles never lost his thick Oxfordshire brogue. On official forms his name became corrupted to Joils, a spelling which was to remain unaltered.

10

# THE FIRST FACTORY

THE same summer saw Thomas widowed in unhappy circumstances.

Jane now lived in a house in New Cross Street, the road in which the Edward Pembertons also resided. Until about July Joseph had continued to share his mother's roof, but her intemperance had become so advanced that it finally drove him from the home. He was twenty-five, ambitious, sensitive. Already two disappointing love affairs lay behind him. Involved in a third, the atmosphere was hardly a favourable one in which to woo a prospective bride. But he remained attached to his mother, and after leaving her, visited her regularly each week.

On Sunday, 18th August, he called in at mid-day. According to the *Advertiser*, which was to report her death in detail, Jane seemed in good health. Joseph thought otherwise, however. In fact, his mother's condition so perturbed him that he considered her insane, and went off to the police station to enquire how he should set about having her put in an asylum.

At two-thirty that afternoon a neighbour of Jane's entered the house and found Jane crouching in a corner of the kitchen in a semi-conscious state. After a while she partly recovered. Apparently she had fallen down, for her left arm was swollen. In reply to a concerned query Jane wished, with touching ambiguity, that "she was hurt nowhere else". Her married daughter, Sarah Pemberton, was sent for, and until about 8 p.m. Jane remained in the hands of relatives, when she was conveyed to Sarah's house. There she deteriorated fast, becoming sensible and wandering by turn. Around midnight she was induced to go upstairs. But the effort proved too much, for no sooner had she done so than an alarming change set in. A doctor was summoned. Though he arrived within ten minutes, he was too late. Jane had died.

Because of the abrupt manner of her death, and again because, according to the *Advertiser*, "disquieting rumours of a vague character" floated about the town, an inquest was held the follow Wednesday at the Royal Hotel. At it the rumours, whatever their nature, were shown to be without foundation. The swelling on the arm was denied by the woman who had laid out the body, and who only found "traces of an old bruise on the hand". The jury returned a verdict to the effect that Jane had died from excessive intemperance, the doctor, on her death certificate, adding a chilling and qualifying "habitual".

A more unlikely couple than Jane and Thomas would have been hard to find. Almost from the start the marriage had failed. Jane was older, and Thomas liked young people, young minds, and particularly young women around him. She drank, and he detested the excesses of alcohol. Child-bearing had broken her health, which he could neither understand, nor even forgive. This had not been the case with his mother, who had reared a larger family in infinitely more adverse circumstances. Intellectually Jane was nowhere near his equal, a gap which had become increasingly pronounced as he became successful.

On Jane's behalf there had been a total lack of social life. Walls covered with sales records, parlours given up to pill-making, had not exactly spelled cosiness. Thomas's infidelities, so at variance with his Bible thumping, were infuriating. One indiscretion had rankled more than most. This was an entry, in pencil, in the family Bible, below the inked-in ones of those of their four children, of "Maggie, b. 3rd August, 1862". At each Sunday reading session his unfaithfulness leapt out at her from the fly-leaf. Jane was also further galled by Thomas's affection for this illegitimate child, and the mother, both of whom he continued to see and care for with the greatest solicitude. Yet, despite the appalling discrepancies of the marriage, despite Jane's unfortunate addiction, she had not been an entirely ineffectual wife. She had provided Thomas with the sheet anchor of a home at a period in his life when it was most vital to have one. Without a base in his mid-twenties, he might have gone on indefinitely combining peddling with casual labour. In Joseph she had given him a more than worthy heir to the business. And she had been musical. It may well have been through her that the strain was transmitted, first to her son, then to the grandson, as yet unborn, who was to give English music a new dimension. For, apart from Tom Templer, it has been impossible to trace any previous musical aptitude in the Beechams; while Templer may have inherited his own streak from his father, Templer history being unknown.

The panacea for disaster had always lain in hard work. Of this there was more than enough at the moment. The two new markets mentioned in the letter to Giles—Africa, and parts of Australia, meant a stepping up of production if that was possible. Nothing was *impossible* to father and son. The turnover, for this domestically unhappy August, was the highest yet recorded, no less than £1,171 5s.! When it is borne in mind that Thomas was still operating from a small workshop, and that he and Joseph managed all the facets of the business between them, the sheer industry exhausts the imagination.

In addition to the manufacture, packaging and desk work, there remained the advertising copy to be written, checked, and filed. The medium attracted Joseph even more than Thomas. But he was impatient for changes, innovations. The slogan, for instance, Worth a Guinea a Box, was capital, but why stick to it doggedly? Why not push others, "A Blessing To All Afflicted", or, "The Right Thing in the Right Place"? And why, whilst on the subject, cling so rigidly to newspaper advertising? What about other forms? Books, puzzles, pamphlets? But it was not the moment, either to coax Thomas, or to startle the general public, with tricks, and Joseph, along with other embryonic advertising geniuses, was obliged to mark time.

He was to go on silently chafing until he had virtual control of the firm. His awe of his father, the habit of deferring to him in everything, instigated in boyhood, was still absolute. Yet in obedience he showed cunning. Instead of submitting to Thomas outright, he would suggest, pretend to concur, retrench quickly if parental wrath exploded, for he could not stand scenes, then bring forward the notion again at a more opportune moment. Make it seem Thomas's own, and so in the end, and without Thomas for a single instant suspecting he had been the victim of an elaborate cat and mouse game, get his own way. Something which William, far less subtle than Joseph, and who argued flatly with his father, seldom did.

Early the following year Thomas, now aged fifty-two, re-married. By an odd coincidence his new bride bore the same name as that of his married daughter—Sarah Pemberton. She was twenty-nine. Why, now that he was free to do so, Thomas did not marry Maggie's mother, who was husbandless, and of whom he remained fond, has not been explained. Or the fact, incredible as it seems, that his Oxfordshire relations were kept in ignorance of this second marriage. His sister Jane had married another farmer very soon after her first husband had died in 1863. A daughter by this second marriage was eight at the time of Thomas's own; she frequently visited Lancashire, and thus heard the family tittle-tattle on both sides. Yet she has never remembered seeing, or hearing anything of Sarah Pemberton, and has been convinced her uncle only married twice. The inference must be drawn that Thomas, for some reason, preferred to keep his marriage quiet; also that Sarah could not have been introduced south.

So far as can be established she was born in Lambeth, her father, a labourer, having moved from Yorkshire about 1840. When Sarah was quite little he had died. Her mother was a nurse, and she herself a milliner. There was also an older brother in the printing trade, who worked locally. For a while the family lived in Commercial Road, since renamed Upper Ground, but at the time of her marriage Sarah was staying in Blackfriars Road, a dreary street of coffee and boarding houses, and stretching from the foot of the bridge for almost two-thirds of a mile.

Thomas now had dealings with six London firms, including, of course, Sutton of Bow Churchyard. From there it was a short walk from Cheapside across the bridge to the New Cut, which ran from Waterloo to Blackfriars. For someone who thirsted after variety, the Cut with its penny gaffs and Sunday market, provided ample diversity. By day the place looked sordid enough, down-at-heel inhabitants swarming around the pawnbroker shops, but at night the bowery theatres and monster gin palaces achieved a tinsel gaiety in the light of winking gas jets. An extra attraction was the Canterbury Music Hall.

Thomas may have met Sarah through her printing brother, or on an inquisitive prowl along the Cut. Their wedding took place quietly on 29th January, 1873, at the parish church of Christ Church, Southwark. At the foot of Blackfriars Bridge, this church had been rebuilt in 1740, the original one having sunk into the ground due to river damp. Thomas much admired its Queen Anne style of architecture, particularly the elegant tower. A friend of the bride's, and the beadle, were witnesses, and unlike her predecessor, Sarah signed the register. Shortly after the ceremony the couple travelled back to Lancashire, settling in Thomas's Westfield Street home. Less than three months later Joseph, also, married.

Unhappily for Joseph the path of true love had been sadly crossed. His earlier attachment for his Hughes cousin had been discouraged, Aunt Jane deeming it unwise for cousins to marry, although her sister Leah's marriage had turned out satisfactorily. Next, Joseph lost his heart to a St. Helens girl, Mary Ellen Westworth, whose father was a plasterer, and whose brother, Thomas, was one of the pioneers of the printing industry in the town. By 1859 he had his own business in Ormskirk Street. Up and coming, the Westworths frowned on the match of one of their members to a man whose father sold pills in the market. That Thomas advertised extensively, and was said to be coining money hand over fist, did not alter matters. Besides, still fresh in everyone's minds, was Jane Beecham's sordid death. Mental derangement in Victorian times was held in terrible fear. Like a troublesome rash it was capable of breaking out again in future generations, and so Joseph's suit was rejected. The following year Mary Ellen married an iron moulder. "She didn't do very well for herself, "and the Westworths were to regret their attitude. The incident, however, provides an example of Thomas's outstanding ability to keep friendships, once made, cemented. Notwithstanding Westworth snobbery, Mary Ellen's brother continued to execute printing orders for him, whilst, on Joseph's own death, it was his firm which printed the catalogue of the sale by auction of Joseph's household furnishings.

Joseph moped, but not for long. Soon he was deeply in love again. In her early twenties, Josephine Burnett had neat features, a small waist and hands, and an abundance of beautiful dark hair. She also possessed an inimitable quality, she was musical. Besides a sweet singing voice she played the piano very prettily. Joseph and his Josephine strummed duets together, and sang songs, in a house in Rigby Street, where they had mutual acquaintances. Josephine's father, William Burnett, was of French extraction, and at this date combined silk dealing with a barber's practice. Ironically enough the Westworths had been instrumental in bringing the pair together, and according to a member of the family "William Burnett had eccentric habits, and he and his wife were talked about a lot locally at the time. Any eccentricity or genius in the descendants was put down to Josephine". The Burnetts must have been odd indeed to have had their quirks noticed in tolerant St. Helens! Far from well off they occupied a small house at the corner of Liverpool Road and Sandfield Crescent, a shabby part of the town since destroyed.

Once again the unfortunate Joseph suffered opposition to proposed marriage plans, this time from Thomas himself. For, despite her humble origins, Josephine had a regal, haughty nature, which more than supported the hints she threw out that patrician blood flowed somewhere in her veins. And though her voice was gentle, and free from any accent, she was extremely exciteable by temperament. Thomas, in reverse of the Mary Ellen argument, felt she was too good for Joseph, who would be better advised to marry someone in his own class. However, for once his son openly defied him, and the tender duet sessions continued unabated. There was a delightful trip to the Isle of Man where a studio portrait was taken. In it Joseph nonchalantly lolls against some ferns, his features, framed between mutton chop whiskers, stoically impassive. Wearing an elegant dress, her lovely hair piled up high, Josephine's attitude is much more intimate, one trusting hand resting on her fiancé's arm.

They were married on 12th August, 1873, at the Parish Church of St. Mary's—inexplicably named this after being reconsecrated in 1816 when the old chapel was enlarged. Since the Beechams were still nonentities in the town the wedding went unreported. It was, in any case, completely overshadowed the same week by that of the vicar's own daughter to a nephew of Viscount Castlemain. Since the bride was "a young lady who had exemplary qualities of head and heart to recommend her" this match was exceedingly popular.

Doting and anonymous the young couple—Joseph was not quite twenty-six—took up residence at 60 Westfield Street. Here three of their ten children were born. Emily in 1874, a child who died, and another girl, Laura, born in January 1877. In many

ways the little Laura was to remind Thomas of his daughter
Jane who had died in 1858, and consequently he became very
attached to her.

The year which saw Joseph a proud father also marked the
end of the green order book. The gross account for 1874 stood at
£16,338 10s. 6d., virtually a six and a half times increase on that
first recorded nine years previously!

Desiring to keep trade in the family, Thomas had been fighting the need of taking on full-time staff. But it was now clear
that if output was to be maintained at its present level, this
policy must be abandoned. In employing help he displayed all
the caution and frugality which had marked his venture into
advertising. A teenager, William Moss, became engaged as a
packer. And an eleven year old boy, Tom Oldham, was employed
in a general capacity, travelling round the countryside with
Thomas, and also putting in a stint of office work. Joseph was
now his father's business manager, his name being mentioned
for the first time in a local directory in 1876. Thomas, of course,
remained chief pharmacist and presiding deity. For approximately three more years this unlikely quartet ran a business
worth sixteens of thousands a year, doing the work between
them which would have kept a dozen men fully occupied twenty-
four hours out of twenty-four!

Frequently cited as a reason for Beecham's success was the
ability of father and son to select suitable employees. In Moss
and Oldham perception was never more aptly displayed.

Not only was William Moss to become works manager, but
he was to be entrusted with the pill formula. This meant he could
be relied upon to the hilt. Till now only Thomas and Joseph
had mixed. The mixer was locked into the mixing room, the
door kept fastened, until the job was completed. Ensuring maximum secrecy the pill ingredients were purchased here, there, and
everywhere, whilst invoices, also, were kept under careful lock
and key. After Thomas and Joseph were dead, Moss perpetuated
this cloak and dagger method, drawing the all endorsing cheque
from the cashier, whilst the actual ingredients were invoiced
under code names understood only by himself and the managing
director. This continued until 1934-5, when it was decided to
take advantage of the government ruling previously given by
the Customs and Excise Authorities that proprietary medicines
sold through chemists only were exempt from the Medicine
Stamp duty, provided their formulas were declared on the con-
tainer. Some time after joining Thomas, Moss became superin-

tendent of the Parish Church Sunday school, and so was responsible for Joseph's playing the organ there.

Oldham worked for Thomas about nine years, when he
became Joseph's coachman, a position he held for life. A staunch
friend of his employers, he was a sympathetic confidante, always
the soul of discretion. Like Joseph he was an excellent judge of
horses, and both men often travelled to Ireland to buy horses for
the Corporation.

If the Beechams were wise in their choice of employees, they
were still cleverer in retaining their services; even despite the fact
that wages given were lower in a town where, glass-making
apart, they were nominal, and when the pound went much
further than it does today. An excuse for parsimony was that
business, nothwithstanding the glittering gross amounts, was
"getting on its feet". And even when it had become obvious to
everyone that it was running, not walking, staff were never
lacking. Not always included in the wages books were the salaries
paid to the hierarchy. But as an example of the extremely low
overheads, in the quarter for June 1891 the staff numbered
seventy-six plus eleven, wages amounting to a mere £68 18s. 2d.
January 1897 was to see staff and wages virtually unaltered,
seventy-four staff plus sixteen, with a total paid for the month
of £76 11s. 4d.

Still, men who had been boys at the firm stayed on, their
children joining them. Moss's son, for instance, succeeded him
at work, dying in harness. Employees stayed from respect, from
contentment with conditions if not wages, and also because of
something less easily defined. For want of a better phrase it might
be called "Beecham mystique". The family had style, pace, a way
of doing things that was somehow different. Today, retainers
who remember Joseph's era, recall the past with nostalgia, and
remain deeply interested in the firm's activities, describing
methods as "Beecham", or "not Beecham". Criticism is not
necessarily implied. Simply, former ways were idiosyncratic.
Indenting themselves on the mind they stamped an indelible
hallmark.

Oldham, perhaps, entertained the greatest sentiment for things
past. His duties, at this date, included helping Thomas in the
market. Years later, surrounded by Joseph's grandeur, he would
sigh half in wonder, half in regret: " 'Ee, but tis not like t' days
wi't' tray." Pills, he said, were then being "got off like hot cakes".
They were. Why then did Thomas, who had no reason to do so,
take up his stand on his fish tub each Saturday? The answer
must be that there was nothing he enjoyed better. It was not

slumming, nor the fad of a wealthy man, nor even the thrift of a careful one. But he liked talking, expounding his herbal theories, and here, unless he indulged in lay preaching, was his sole pulpit. Within a few years, however, he was to stop selling in the market. A slightly infra dig occurrence taking place about this time, may have helped change his ways.

One Saturday he was setting up his pitch, fixing a challenging placard to the barrel, which on this occasion bore the provocative caption: "Who Did It?" Closely watching him was a band of small boys, including James Sexton, a future borough M.P. According to Sexton, who loved repeating the story, he and his companions managed to loosen the majority of hoops round the barrel, even prizing several away. At last Thomas mounted his "platform". He was just warming up to his subject, when the anticipated crash came, and he vanished from view. All that remained above was the mocking query, "Who Did It?" The fact that Thomas never operated from a stall in the market is another instance of how much he treasured the milestones of his pursuit. Things were only dispensed with when they were *outmoded*, and a fish tub probably attracted more attention.

In 1876 Thomas acquired two more cottages in Westfield Street. He also became owner of 53 Rigby Street, the house where Joseph and Josephine had warbled their duets. Some time that year he moved into it. Three up and three down like his old home, this tenement house had a scullery, but no bathroom, whilst the privy was situated at the bottom of the back yard. Today No. 69, it is almost exactly as it was when Thomas lived there. The hall varnished dark brown with cherubs inset (a favourite design), and the stove in the back room still with its tap at the side for filling kettles. By the following year Thomas additionally owned Nos. 54-57, and also more property in Westfield Street. But his present address was presumably only meant to be a stop-gap, for either at the end of 1876, or the beginning of the new year, he arranged for a house to be built more in keeping with his improved conditions, one approximately half way up Croppers Hill.

Happiest when operating on several fronts at once, Thomas was also in the throes of erecting his first factory. Situated between Westfield Street and Silver Street, entry was gained by a high arched gateway via a third one, in Water Street. A long, single storied building, with no bottom windows, but several large upper ones, it resembled a barn, and had a conical tower round which it was possible to stroll and take a birds' eye view of the packing sheds at the rear. The number of staff employed at this time is unknown, but six years later some eighteen people were engaged, the total weekly wages for September being £14 4s. 6d. Walter Andrews, now with the firm as the first works manager, received the highest paid salary, £2 6s., increased to £3 10s. the following year. Moss was receiving 28s., whilst the lowest recorded wage was 5s. 6d. a week, only four more shillings than Thomas had got when he had started out to work more than fifty years before!

One entry in the book explains why the Beechams were held in such high esteem by employees. A worker was paid 2s. a week whilst he was ill, and cared for for seven weeks, a rare procedure at a period when sick pay was unknown, and there was no National Health Service. Thomas, however, with memories of earlier ill health, was sympathetic towards ailing staff, visiting them personally in their homes at such times. It was possibly at this date that the system was devised whereby employees of Beecham's contributed a penny a week to a fund which entitled them, in case of accident or illness, to receive medical attention in their homes. And it was a point of honour that they got their jobs back upon recovery.

Conditions imposed in this first factory were as stringent as those Thomas had always set himself. Punctuality. A time-keeper's lodge stood outside the entrance, and heaven help the late arrival! Hard work. The hours stretched from 6 a.m. to 6 p.m. with no Saturday afternoons off, and no holidays. Cleanliness. Floors and benches were kept scrubbed by the workers, who also had to be immaculately tidy, and were not encouraged to talk on the job.

A house adjoining the factory went up at the same time, and was completed by 1877. At the corner of Arthur Street, it was a substantial one, the gross value being shown in the local Rate Book at £50. Chief features were the stables, and a large dining-room, and into it when it was ready moved the Joseph Beechams with their two little daughters. After the poky cottage where they had started married life it was wonderfully spacious and luxurious. And it was just as well it was next to the factory. "I used to work till midnight", Joseph was to say of this era, "and rise each morning at five, to be at my desk by five-thirty".

Thomas transferred to his own new home, Hill House, during the summer of 1877. His son, William, accompanied him, but not his wife, Sarah. She had been ill for some time, and in fact suffered from several of the hallucinations which had afflicted Jane Beecham. She also screamed a good deal at night. At the beginning of May indefinite uroemia set in. For three weeks Sarah endured this, before dying on the 24th, aged thirty-three. Her husband was present at the death. Looking down at the still young form of his wife the thought must have occurred to him that, fortunate as he was with business, where affairs of the heart were concerned, the dice were loaded against him. Despite this he was to make one more bid for marital bliss.

Thomas continued as the owner of 53 Rigby Street, which, by a strange twist of fate, was to be occupied for a brief space by Mary Ellen Westworth, now Mrs. Wilson. When she left, William Moss moved in as tenant. After he became general works manager at Beecham's, a more agreeable residence was built for him by the firm elsewhere in the town. For a short time Mary Ellen's printing brother lived in No. 53, when it became the permanent home of the Oldhams.

In common with many philanderers Thomas had difficulty in shaking off the past. For some years after he had left the house young women were apt to knock on the door and enquire if "Old Mr. Beecham is at the works today?"

## 11

# A TEMPESTUOUS UNION

ENSCONCED in his brand new home Joseph felt inspired to take increasing interest in a town which could now boast a cottage hospital, a rambling club, and evening classes for the serious minded in its Science and Art Department. A town which had been given parliamentary representation in 1884. Which was to acquire county borough status five years later, bloomed with parks, and had a flourishing debating society. St. Helens was becoming subjugated beyond recognition. If additional proof of its respectability was needed, six thousand people had signed the pledge following a temperance campaign in 1882. Perhaps, wisely, local history has not recorded how many kept it, but at least the signing had gone on for six whole days! And, warming the cockles of Joseph's heart, *Messiah* had been performed annually there for over twenty years.

Joseph's many activities were bringing him into contact with important people who could help promote his ambitions. A useful introduction was one at the Cycling Club. Charles Rowed, an Anglo-American, besides being an authority on pewter, shared Joseph's enthusiasm for advertising. The two men would discuss its potentialities for hours on end.

After his son's marriage Thomas had increased his salary, and the outward trappings of this raise were servants, horses, and a landau. Joseph travelled extensively for the firm, was often abroad, and from these trips he brought home innumerable trophies. Bric-a-brac, busts, marble pieces, and beautiful cut glass vases now decorated his home. His pretty wife was an admirable hostess, finicky almost to a fault. Dispensing with the services of a housekeeper, she liked to put the finishing touches to meals, and personally supervise the table arrangements. Able now, also, to give free rein to his artistic inclinations, Joseph's upright piano was presently joined by an organ he had built into one of the rooms. Soft, or easy living, he enjoyed, yet he had inherited Thomas's streak of economy. The pounds looked after themselves because the pennies were always excellently preserved. Once, when playing cards with some friends, a half-penny rolled off the table. Proceedings were delayed for nearly an hour whilst Joseph grovelled on all fours looking for it. His children were given gun metal watches long before being treated to silver or gold varieties.

Conversely, as Joseph's life assumed broader and loftier dimensions, Thomas's stayed stubbornly modest. Hill House on Cropper's Hill was detached, and for the first time since settling in Lancashire Thomas virtually lived apart from the artisan class, the joiners, labourers, and petty tradesmen who had hitherto comprised his neighbours. But his style was unchanged. He still wore paper collars, because, as he said, he had used them so long, he was unable to adjust himself to linen ones. Relatives who did not mind roughing it were put up, but he never formally entertained. To ride in his own carriage had been his greatest ambition, but now that he could afford to do so, he preferred to walk. The habit was unbreakable. Carriages, in any case, made him fretful, restless. They were too slow, and the only ones which satisfied his craving for perpetual motion were the railway sort. A pony and trap driven by Oldham, were kept in Joseph's stable. Though proud of these, Thomas used them solely for business purposes, Oldham transporting him to, and from, the station. This was the only personal carriage Thomas ever rode in. The strange voice behind the Oxfordshire hedge had spoken correctly; only its listener had modified ambition.

Built of brick and red Ashley stone, with some eleven rooms including a wash-house, Hill House was much pleasanter than his Rigby Street home. Double-fronted, with a small garden in front, arched upper windows and a pseudo-Norman porch gave it a faintly churchy air, enhanced by a stone plaque over the entrance of a saintly looking child, an arm round a lion, surrounded by other animals. Below this the inscription read : "And a little child shall lead them." Also gracing the door was the St. Helens coat of arms, and town motto which Thomas, with his faith in herbs and all natural products of the soil, might have inspired. "Out of the earth came light." Fruit and vegetables were cultivated in an extensive garden at the rear of the building.

The Beechams were coming up fast. Too quickly for some people, and Thomas appears to have felt himself the victim of jealousy, as he had been at Wigan, since he had recourse to discarded rhetoric in an advertisement in *Jackson's Oxford Journal.* What, he demanded, was Truth? It was, apparently, "more solid than the granite rocks; it is the richest coin of the purest metal free from alloy of every description. The shafts of envy will not deface it, neither will the shots of prejudice enter it. It is surrounded on all sides by a thousand foes, but each and all, without exception, are mute beneath its piercing glance". In fact, and thank goodness, it was as solid as Beecham's Pills. So much for Mr. Envy and Mr. Prejudice, still trying to cramp success.

This was in 1879, an eventful year for father and son.

On 29th April, Josephine gave birth to a baby boy. Joseph was thrilled, and this time there was no departure from tradition regarding names, the child being called Thomas, after his paternal grandfather. He had, of course, much to live up to in the way of initiative and industry, but since April was the reputed month for geniuses, his birth date augured well. Thomas senior, with his strong dynastic sense, was every bit as pleased as the parents. Now an heir to the heir of the business was ensured.

Thomas still visited Oxfordshire regularly, never letting more than a year elapse without seeing his mother. Joseph went also, taking his children to stay with Aunt Jane, as he had done in boyhood. Jane had been able to remain at the Hogshaw farm, which would pass to a Hughes son when he was twenty-one. After this she moved to a new farm at Granborough. Her second husband was not a very able farmer, having a philosophical, rather than a practical turn of mind, and once again Thomas generously stepped into the financial breach, helping his sister with her second family. Joseph occasionally called in on Granny

Mary, Thomas's third wife, with maid

Thomas Beecham at Mursley Hall

Thomas Beecham, his son William, and his wife Mary outside Mursley Hall

Sarah Ann, Thomas Beecham's daughter

Morris. At almost eighty she had become very shrivelled. On seeing her for the first time a grand-daughter fled shrieking from the room, supposing her to be a witch. A photograph taken of Sarah in old age does vaguely suggest one, but a witch with a tremendous relish for life. The caved in face is filled with energy, and sly humour. A charming touch is the posy of violets held between the inordinately long fingers. In spite of her years she was intensely active, and like her eldest son took immense interest in the antics of her fellow human beings. Warm summer days found her shelling peas on a chair taken into the garden, the better to observe who passed by in the lane beyond. The grey stone cottage was now unnaturally quiet. Both the half-sisters had married, and besides her husband, Granny Morris had only her bachelor son, Charles, to care for. And at the beginning of August, Charles, a labourer, died of spinal disease at the early age of thirty-one.

Thomas went to the funeral, conducted at Curbridge which now had its own pantiled church. Unlike many of the Beecham dead the grave was given a headstone, Thomas doubtless contributing to this.

Leaving the funeral, and on Banbury station, Thomas met "the prettiest woman he ever saw". Mrs. Mary Sawell was returning from the wedding of an aunt, and soon the two, evidently with time to spare between trains, were deep in conversation.

Mrs. Sawell was different from any other woman of Thomas's acquaintance in that she had an air of authority, and was smartly dressed. Under her hat rich, dark curls marched across a creamy forehead. If the mouth was a trifle too wide in the strong-willed, oval face, this flaw was more than compensated by her large, fiery eyes, whilst her figure was both shapely and well-proportioned. For her part Mary Sawell was amused, but drawn, to the scruffy little man who talked so knowledgeably on every subject under the sun. If he had not told her he had money, she would never have guessed it. His clothes were prehistoric—but the personality was compelling. Almost against her will she found herself hypnotized.

Thomas's courtships were apt to be whirlwind. The two left the station together, and spent the night in Banbury. Utterly captivated, Thomas implored Mary to marry him. But at first she refused. Everything was against the union. Their difference in ages, she was not quite twenty-eight to his fifty-nine. Used to refinements she was not sure if she could endure Thomas's manners which bordered on the uncouth. Her relations lived in the south, and despite her chic she was a country lover. Her hesitation fanned Thomas's ardour. He grew reckless, promising Mrs. Sawell anything if she would only be his wife. Money, jewellery, even horses, since she was fond of riding. And in the end, and as she was to frankly admit, money spoke louder than prudence. On 2nd September, 1879, a month after their fateful encounter, the two were married at Christ Church, Eccleston. Both Joseph and William violently disapproved, mainly for the reasons originally put forward by their new stepmother. They were to have the grim satisfaction of watching the union almost immediately disintegrate.

For it seemed that for once Thomas was not absolute master in his own household, his bride being as forceful a character as he was himself. To date hers had been a packed life, indeed, almost a unique one for a woman in Victorian times. Most of the information about Mary has been given by a maid, Mrs. Bennett, whom she was later to employ. Not all of it can be checked, but on Mrs. Bennett's own admission Mary was extremely honest. "I think you can rely on everything she told me, as she was very truthful, even if it went against herself."

Born Mary Putt, Mrs. Sawell's father was a shoemaker, turned road contractor. For some reason she had been brought up by an aunt in Canterbury, and not amongst her Oxfordshire relations. At one time this aunt was said to have acted as housekeeper to the archbishop there, and consequently Mary was given a background and standards quite different from those which would ordinarily have been her lot.

It was at Canterbury that she met her first two husbands. When only seventeen she had married an Irish major. Soon after the wedding the husband was posted to India. Not accompanying him on the troopship, she never saw him again, for shortly after setting foot on that continent he was murdered by a native.

Next Mary married a Captain in the 16th Lancers. This marriage, too, was to be short-lived, for within eighteen months he had died of tuberculosis. Apparently Mary had a *penchant* for the military, her new love being a medical officer, Colonel (then probably Captain) Hector. He had waxed moustachios, was handsome in a glassy-eyed, full-blooded way, and the pair became inseparable. Alas for male fickleness! Hector adored his little darling, but the army even more. One day, in evident distress, he told Mary he had been ordered abroad by his regiment. If it was not too much to expect, did she think she could wait until his return? She would, and gladly. However, no sooner had her fiancé sailed away than a friend informed Mary that Hector had *volunteered*, not been dispatched. Piqued, Mary who was capricious and high-spirited, broke off the engagement. On the rebound she married a Mr. Sawell. Nothing is known of him, except that, by the time she met Thomas, she was again widowed.

After the dignity of Canterbury, the leafy freshness of Oxfordshire, it was hardly to be expected that Mary would welcome the industrial north. She did not. From the start she loathed everything about St. Helens. The chemical odours encloaking the town. The hideous monotony of the brick dwellings, the smoke and grime. Still expanding rapidly at all points of the compass, it was becoming increasingly difficult to take a healthy stroll without first tramping through miles of ribbon streets. The newly-formed Tramways Company was, two years later, to be obliged to run an hourly horse-drawn service to Prescot, whilst by the following spring, lines were to be laid to the countrified district of Denton's Green. The shape of the village which had still been visible when Thomas had settled there two decades previously was now irretrievably lost.

This was bad enough. But worse than urban dinginess was Thomas's behaviour, which frayed Mary's nerves. Once snared, he neglected her. Accustomed to being spoiled by menfolk, she was chagrined to find that his over-ruling passion in life was work. To *that* she must always play second fiddle! Not only did it absorb him each and every day, but he would disappear for weeks at a time, not telling her where he was going, or when she might expect him back. Before marrying him she had realized that he lived crudely and cared nothing for appearances. Nevertheless, she was unprepared for his total lack of social life, irregular meals, and the way he wolfed down his food when she *could* get him to sit down to it. She complained he refused to compromise, but laid down the law in everything. Since she was a law to herself arguments abounded. Occasionally Thomas actually found himself worsted. This was even more annoying than Mary's obstinacy. Here was no illiterate wife, or one whose poor health made her indifferent to putting up a fight. Instead, he had on his hands a woman whose tongue could be as cutting as his own, who had known, and insisted upon, a genteel mode of living, and who had the temerity to assume that money was a commodity to be spent. Gossiping as she did, Mary learnt details of Thomas's first wife, about whom he had confided nothing. And what she heard in a town where "everyone was related" worried her, so that she began to be more than ever uncertain of the man she had married.

Yet for almost a year she endured St. Helens. Though he kept her short of ready cash, Thomas had given her the other gifts promised before the wedding, including hunters. A few more compensations existed. Mary got on well with Joseph and William, who, at thirty-one and twenty-four, were her own generation. Joseph's home, particularly, with its comfort and servants, attracted her, and there she could relax. Fond of children she became a favourite in the nursery. With Josephine she was less at ease. Free-spoken like herself, Josephine could be every bit as variable. Sometimes she would welcome visitors with open arms. At others, bypassing her nice drawing-room, she swept them, for no apparent reason, on to the kitchen, where they were given jam-making to do. The truth was that a highly strung nature was already beginning to crack under the strain of too many births occurring far too rapidly.

Mary's Canterbury training also opened up other circles for her. She hunted with members of the Pilkington family with whom she became friendly, and who pitied her because of the incompatability of her marriage. This infuriated Thomas. He could never forget that a Pilkington had sat on the bench when he had been bound over to keep the peace in 1861. In order to stop her riding he locked up Mary's horses in the paddock. Crisis followed crisis. "It would have been all right if she was one of the hard sort," Mrs. Bennett has averred. "She could have got all she wanted out of him and then left him just like that. But she was both sensitive and high principled."

Principles or no principles the moment arrived when Mary could not stand the north a moment longer. She announced her intention of leaving it for good. Without much protest Thomas acquiesced. Far from well, after years of remorseless application to work he was approaching physical collapse. Doctors, whom, in a desperate measure, he consulted, urged him in no uncertain terms to seek rest. It was especially advisable, for his lungs' sake that he find a more wholesome climate in which to live. Fortunately the time could not have been more opportune. The firm offered no problems. Joseph, Walter Andrews, Moss, and Oldham were more than capable of running it in his absence. A temporary absence, naturally, since retirement at sixty was out of the question. Commuting between the north and the south had never presented difficulties, and when he was better he could travel to Lancashire at least once a month to keep an eye on things. On the whole he was bolstered, rather than discouraged, by the turn of events, and sometime in 1880 he and Mary journied to Oxfordshire to search for a likely home. With a factory and two houses to his credit, Thomas had been bitten by the

building bug, and nothing but a house erected to his own speci-
fications would suit him. Schemes and plans were also a way of
passing enforced idleness.

Land was eventually purchased adjoining the churchyard at
Mursley, a small village near Winslow, in Buckinghamshire. It
had the advantage of being central to their joint relations, whilst
at Bletchley, less than ten miles away, there was a station. Some
three hundred acres were bought, and building commenced that
year, or early the next. Whilst it was going on the Beechams
stayed in the village.

With his enthusiasm for any project he undertook, Thomas
was on the spot most days, chivvying and bullying the workmen. Once, growing impatient, he asked the foreman how
matters were progressing. Well enough, apparently, though to
be strictly honest the pace could be a little faster. The same
thought had occurred to Thomas. Next morning he rushed over
with a fistful of pills, handing one to each man on the job. For
a week he kept away, then he was back, wanting to know, with
a sardonic smile, how the men had fared. "Fine!" "Never felt
better, guv'nor", they muttered. Except for a small fellow who
swore petulantly that he had been so ill he was laid up for two
days. At which Thomas roared with laughter, declared he was
the only truthful chap amongst them, and recommended he take
a week's holiday.

By the late summer of 1881 Hill House had been let, and the
Beechams were installed at Mursley Hall. The place cost approximately £11,000, a large sum for those days, though this figure
probably included the land, and twelve cottages Thomas erected
in the village, and into the brickwork of which he had his initials
pricked. They also topped the weather vane which surmounted
the red brick pile of Mursley Hall. Solid and rather ugly, there
were good-sized stables, and beyond the elaborate front porch a
Monkey Puzzle tree sawed the air. The long drive, part of which
flanked the churchyard, afforded Thomas coveted privacy, and
in time he developed a small farm in the grounds.

For a year or two the Beechams were reasonably happy at
Mursley. Mary saw a good deal of her relations, and hunted
with the Bucks Stag Hounds. She had several friends in the district, one of whom was a schoolteacher. When not at the hospital in London, William stayed, and Joseph put in regular
appearances. As his health improved Thomas devoted more and
more time to the activities of his little estate. He found immense
satisfaction in playing yeoman farmer. In, recollecting the past,
employing labouring help. Above all he liked watching the wind

gaily rotate his initials on the weather vane, in reflecting on
that fact that his name was now known far beyond the confines
of the south. And he enjoyed coming home to roost amongst
his southern relatives, caught up in the minutiae of sisters',
brothers', nieces', nephews' and cousins' doings. Family affairs
were much to the fore. In the April after moving in his stepfather died. The same year a baby girl, Josephine, was born to
the Joseph Beechams. Birth, and then death, striking this family
in the space of a few months, for, on Christmas Day, the small
grand-daughter Laura, who had reminded Thomas so much of his
daughter Jane, died, aged almost five. She was buried in Non-
conformist ground in a red and grey marble vault on 29th
December at Dent Green Cemetery. Thereafter Christmas, in
that household, too often came to be an occasion for fear and
agitation, instead of a happy festival. A legend sprang up
amongst the more superstitious Beechams that their members
tended to die between September and March. On average, of
course, this was possible in any large family, but to date Thomas's
maternal grandmother, his Aunt Mary Templer, his father, and
a daughter had all died between these months. Seven years later,
in February, Uncle William of Kidlington died at ninety-three,
working almost up to the last, Thomas's daughter, Sarah Ann
Pemberton was to die on 24th December, 1893, and sister Jane
would pass away in September 1909.

More trouble came the following year. Thomas's son-in-law,
Edward Pemberton, with whom he had some building transactions in St. Helens, was declared bankrupt. This necessitated
going north to sort things out. Back at the firm Thomas came
under the old, heady spell of pill-making again. The mixing room,
the bustle and excitement of getting off orders, advertising copy
—he had not realized how much he had been missing everything.
Mursley Hall . . . a farm . . . amateur squirearchy . . . these
were quiet pursuits, and as such circumscribed by boredom. The
factory was his life. And so, gradually, he picked up the dropped
threads again, began to travel around the countryside. To absent
himself from home for days, then weeks together. Once more
Mary was left alone.

At first she did not mind. She had enough to occupy her. If
unromantically worded, Thomas at least wrote her letters. But
after a while, and as he stayed away with greater frequency, she
grew peeved, then downright nervous. The house was dreadfully isolated; the long drive especially, frightened her, particularly when walking up it alone in the evenings. Servants slept in
only spasmodically. One of Mary's grievances was that Thomas's

amorality made it impossible to keep maids for long. Even before they had taken occupation he had arranged to meet a cook there to inspect culinary installations. But "the appointment had been for the wrong purpose", and the woman had to be dismissed. Mary's schoolteacher friend was persuaded to stay with her. And when at last Thomas did choose to return home his wife's relief not unnaturally, took the form of outbursts of pent-up temper.

Inevitably their relationship deteriorated. Another of Mary's accusations was that Thomas was vindictive, and "took swipes at her dogs, knowing that she was an animal lover". This he would never have done had they been used for sheep, but he did have contempt for pet dogs. He also locked up her hunters again, but she out-witted him by means of waving a dish of corn in their direction, and tempting them to jump over the gate. An incident occurring at Mursley, both illustrates Thomas's "dark" side, and his venom when crossed. One day a horse threw him. In a cold rage he remounted it, driving and driving the animal till it dropped down dead under him.

Thomas continued to ration Mary with spending money, but once more she proved resourceful. Her husband kept enormous quantities of bank notes stuffed away in a rolltop desk. His wife had a duplicate key made, and helped herself to whatever she wanted when she liked, Thomas seeming none the wiser. "His only aim," according to Mrs. Bennett, being "in making money, but he wasn't interested when he got it."

A taunt of Mary's, galling to a Congregationalist, was to tell Thomas he looked like a Methodist parson. In fact, in a photograph taken on horseback outside Mursley Hall, Thomas, in a shapeless jacket, his hard black hat rammed on his head, definitely resembles one. He glares across at Mary, also on horseback. She stares irritably down. In the doorway William lounges, blinking in the light. The impression prevails that no-one really wanted this picture executed, only the horses having their heads conveniently turned towards the camera.

Two other photographs both taken around this time, do better justice to the Beechams. By the porch, Mary, again in riding habit, and looking moody and magnificent, holds her steed's head. Thomas is without his unflattering hat, so that his impressive brow is fully exposed. The face, surrounded by a fungus of beard, is shrewd and calculating, whilst two, fantastically tapered fingers rest on his hip.

Mary was to state that Thomas was never physically unkind to her. It was his mental sadism which could be supreme. For him her worst offence must have been in her revelation to the

world at large of the contents of his costive pill. After all his
efforts to keep these a closely guarded secret this was unforgiv-
able !

Matters eventually reached a peak in a highly dramatic
manner. Returning home after one of his prolonged absences,
Thomas decided that Mary looked unwell. He put his fingers into
his waistcoat pocket and produced two pills. Carefully he
watched her swallow them, then tore off the same night, staying
away for six whole weeks. During this period Mary became very
ill indeed. For days she lay in bed, and afterwards swore that only
the consumption of champagne and chicken had kept her alive.
Convinced Thomas had intended poisoning her, she was now
terrified to be left alone with him. Imported more or less permanently into the house was the obliging schoolteacher friend, who
slept with Mary on Thomas's visits, at such times the women
keeping the bedroom door well locked. Defeated, outraged,
Thomas stormed, but without avail; the door stayed shut.

Soon after this came the break-up. They had been married four
or five years, and it was from both sides. Mary could not stand
Thomas's persistent infidelities—which, in fairness to him, if
she refused to consummate the marriage, she must have
provoked. She, herself, was a difficult person to live with, her own
relations finding her restless and changeable, "giving with one
hand and taking away with the other". Because of this temperament she made many enemies, and these she harassed with solicitors' letters.

Following a separation, a settlement was made. Highly sus-
picious of her husband Mary prevailed upon her trustees to refuse to accept a cheque, and Thomas was obliged to pay her in
bank notes. However, in a clear case of one-upmanship, he
arranged that she could not touch the principal settled on her
until his death, lest she come back to him for more. Mary's
claims were backed by Joseph and William, who felt she was
right to leave Thomas, and who remained on friendly terms with
their stepmother.

Mary's story was to have a happy sequel. Colonel Hector,
whom she had jilted, and who was now in England, re-entered
her life. She had lost none of her affection for this errant soldier,
and went to live with him in a villa in Banbury Road. Although
it would have suited her, Mary refused to divorce Thomas, saying she never wanted to see him treat another wife in the same
fashion. As it happened she did not marry her Colonel until
about a year after Thomas's death. By then Hector was sixty-six,
and she fifty-five. She developed a habit of cycling to various

villages where she sold eggs, and since she wore bloomers for this, and was one of the first women in the vicinity to do so, acquired a reputation for eccentricity. As late as the turn of the century trousers, for women, were still being hotly debated. She survived her husband by a number of years, the last seven of which saw her hopelessly crippled by arthritis. Nursed by a neighbour, the latter, on Mary's instructions, destroyed all the letters in her possession, including, unfortunately, those Thomas had written her. It was while she was living with Colonel Hector that Mary employed Mrs. Bennett as a maid. And it was to Mrs. Bennett that she confided the legend that "Thomas promised a shepherd on his deathbed he would patent the recipe for his pills to provide an income for the shepherd's wife". Mrs. Bennett never heard the name of the shepherd, only that he had lived at Curbridge.

This maid never actually met Thomas, so all that she knew was therefore secondhand. Nevertheless, she has given a pen portrait of him which, though perforcedly biased, and arrived at by hearsay, confirms much that people who personally knew him have said, and which is wonderfully graphic. "He wasn't a man who cared for comfort or a home. He didn't care what he drank, or what he ate, or what he ate it with. . . . He was very eccentric. His only recreation was women, not because he wanted to get them exactly, but because he enjoyed their company. He was utterly single-minded about his pills and his sole recreation. He didn't care for a social life and had no desire to rise in the social scale. He was what he was, and people could take him or leave him. He was a little man and he had a terrible temper!"

The piece about Thomas not wanting to get women so much as merely enjoying their company, is less ambiguous than it sounds. Women were as natural as the air he breathed, the pill odours he inhaled. He had been abundantly petticoated in early childhood. For nearly three years he had basked in his mother's undivided attention. He was almost ten before the first brother was born, his adoring sisters had a new male playmate. Women had nursed, fussed, favoured, and looked up to him; he had shone in their eyes. Highly-sexed, he had only to crook his little finger to have them come running, whilst in advancing age money was an irresistible attraction. Yet with or without love-making, he liked them about. In a way they were an equivalent of the notes locked up in the roll-top desk. A vital function of life, but in the last analysis not the most important. That was work.

Mary's obstinacy clipped Thomas's matrimonial wings. Though it is doubtful if he would have re-married had she divorced him, he was to say to one other that, had he met her years before, he would have been a better man.

Meanwhile, at Mursley Hall, Thomas was being made to swallow some of his own medicine. Without companionship the days dragged as heavily as they had once done for Mary. True, the clan kept him occupied. He went weekly to see his mother. His brothers had been set up on farms, and he derived pleasure from visiting and advising them. He was still undisputed chief of the Oxfordshire-born Beechams . . . and yet, with the passage of time, something had gone wrong. Though uncomplicated in the sense that, unlike Joseph, he did not have a dual personality, Thomas, in common with most individuals, could be more than one person to several people. To his immediate family he was difficult, demanding, hot-tempered. To the southern relations he would always be easier. "Our Tom" who, in the best tradition, had left home, raised them all from the ignominy of poverty, who was unendingly munificent, and whose faults of temperament, since they knew them so well, and shared a good many, could be tolerated, but not feared. To the new generations emerging from amongst them, however, to the critical young, Thomas was something quite different again. A notorious philanderer, who ludicrously chose to forget his age. Dreadfully opinionated, he dressed like a tramp, was often embarrassingly crude, and lectured them obsessively on the value of herbs and mathematics. Small fry, calling at his mausoleum, were in danger of being sat at a table and made to do the rule of three (the principle which teaches how to find a fourth proportional number to three others which are given), or they were set conundrums and riddles, instead of being given the run of the grounds. Admittedly, Uncle Tom slipped sovereigns into their hands, helped educate them, heaped their parents with presents, but he could also be perversely penny-pinching. Ungrateful, they muttered, or were openly rebellious. A male relative, sent to a good boarding school, protested he was given insufficient pocket money. When Thomas, who hated to be asked for anything, turned cloth ears to this plea, the boy, aided by the school gardener, escaped over the garden wall. Two other female relations, heard giggling about Thomas's affairs in his own house, were surprised not to be invited again. And when yet another, clearly on the make, stipulated she needed two lengths of material for a dress, Thomas roared at her, "What, a little thing like you needing all that stuff?"

Mentally rebuffed by insurbordination, his seigneur's grasp

slipping, Mursley inevitably lost its attraction. Thomas's thoughts began to dwell increasingly on the future. And there was no doubt about it, this was where it had always been, in the north.

The year was 1884. A great deal had been happening at the firm. Virtually in control for the last five years Joseph had taken the business to vertiginous heights. These would become mere molehills in comparison with what lay ahead. But first, and before further progress could be made, one or two things had to be discarded. Notably Thomas's first, barn-style factory. Apart from the fact that it had become too small, its main fault lay *in* its plainness.

## 12

# MECCA OF GLOBULES

BEECHAM fortunes had soared during the years 1864-75. The next decade was to prove one of even greater transition. By the time it was over the thriving family concern would have grown into a fully-fledged commercial enterprise, splendidly housed, with an advertising campaign of unprecedented magnitude already unleased.

Some extent of the scope of business is indicated by the fact that approximately four hundredweight of pills were being turned out of the cutting machine every day. A memorandum for handbills scribbled by Thomas on 3rd December, 1884, requested the *first million* (his italics) no later than Christmas. A tall order for any company! But possibly this one was galvanized by Thomas's decision "to give you the order for printing of the same the next two years altho I have a quotation in a little lower than yours but knowing you do the work well it can in future be depended on". Nineteen staff were employed at this period. By January of the new year this had risen to twenty-six, a number swollen to fifty-seven by August.

More man-power, plus ever-expanding business, necessitated larger working space, and so the old factory was completely razed, and a new pillery erected in its place. A complicated pro-

cess of demolition and construction which went on for approximately five years. During it temporary premises were acquired in
nearby Lowe Street, where local inhabitants have it that Thomas's
ghost stalks, his conscience, because of his womanizing, pricking
him. How on earth Thomas, but especially Joseph, managed to
keep tight control of so many activities in these hectic years,
remains an inpenetrable miracle. But to stupefying Beecham
energy was lashed experience. In a lesser degree they had dealt
with the same problem nearly ten years before, when the now
obsolete factory had gone up, and father and son had also built,
and moved into, new homes.

Costing £30,000 the factory had three imposing frontages
opening onto the corners of Waterloo Street, Westfield Street,
and Silver Street. Built in the Queen Anne style of architecture
Thomas had admired in Christ Church, Southwark, it was, apart
from this, Joseph's dream, Joseph's conception, and Joseph's glory.
And since he combined the practical with the aesthetic to a
superlative degree, it was the last word in efficiency and elegance.

Inasmuch as it dipped, the site presented a problem. But over-
coming this a clock tower, rising 150 feet, provided an excellent
landmark, and quickly became famous. Pilkington employees (a
cause for complacency) set their watches by it, and whenever a
discrepancy existed between it, and the town hall clock,
Beecham's time was preferred by the townsfolk. Costing just
under a thousand pounds, it had four dials. Originally only three
were intended, but Joseph, ". . . believing it to be of great benefit
to Greenbank, the poorer part of the town . . . made the addition
of a fourth especially for them". Exceptionally musical were its
Cambridgeshire chimes. Striking the quarterly and hourly inter-
vals they could be heard over a distance of several miles.

The factory had a dynastic, as well as a graceful, exterior. Cut
into the stone above the main entrance was the omniscient mono-
gram, BEECHAM. Health and Beauty, in flowing robes, upheld
a garland on which was emblazoned the priceless slogan. The
three generations were represented by Joseph's bust over the
porch, flanked, to his right, by his father's, to his left, by that
of his son, Thomas, the boy wearing a sailor suit. Other figures
in relief adorned the sides of the building. Joseph's wife, complete with ear-rings, a fringe, and looking remarkably youthful;
and their three daughters, Emily, Josephine, and Edith in a
cot, the last baby having been born in 1884. Though the Joseph
Beechams had four more children, their images were never perpetuated, since the sculptor who did the frieze of heads vanished

from the bosom of his family before the work could be completed. He was never heard of again, and his disappearance remained a mystery to everyone concerned.

Though not having been given pride of place on the porch, Thomas was to be commemorated elsewhere, a somewhat pious bust in white marble being duly executed, and placed in the hall. The latter was unusually grand. Hung with magnificent electric light pendants—the factory was the first to be installed with electricity in St. Helens—it had a beautiful mosaic floor, and a richly carved balustrade. Into it Joseph, rather in the manner of a proud housewife cluttering up her parlour, arranged fine walnut furniture, palms, ferns, marble statues, and *objets d'arts* culled from his extensive wanderings.

All over the building in unlikely as well as obvious places, fittings and furnishings were of the best and most luxurious quality. According to the *British Journal of Commerce* the engine room, housing a 20 h.p. engine with dynamo for supplying the whole works with electricity, was "more like some scene from the Arabian nights, then a factory". With a ceiling of ornamental wood, walls decorated with Minton tiles, electric lights shaded with porcelain globes "of a beautiful design", even the leather belting was ornamental. There was also a 4 h.p. engine with dynamo which supplied only the offices when the remainder of the works were closed—the Beechams, withal, being mindful of economy. A smaller engine house with a 12 h.p. engine served to drive the machinery.

Though his retirement was still well in the future, Thomas was being inexorably pushed aside by his son's generation. This was evident in a far more touching manner than that of the position of his bust over the entrance. A museum in the basement contained many of his inventions, which if they did not exactly gather dust, unthinkable in a Beecham institute, at least collected allegorical moss. However, he had been the mainspring, and it was from his outmoded ideas that fresh contraptions were evolved, an important one being a pill-counting machine. Years before Thomas had constructed a simple, but ingenious contrivance for this. Resembling a butter-pat, it contained as many grooves as there were pills in each box. When put amongst them the pills came up to full. It was then emptied into a funnel under the end of which the pill boxes were passed by hand. To his indignation the contrivance had been copied by a rival pill-maker. But later, either Walter Andrews, the works manager, or Charles Rowed, now Joseph's secretary, improved on it with a still better machine. Operated by a water motor, and requiring even less manual labour, it was capable of counting and filling three thousand boxes of pills a day. Rowed also invented a machine called a picker, specifically for testing the perfection of the pill's shape. Both devices were considered unique in the country, and visitors were not permitted to approach them too closely. Neither Thomas or Joseph intended to be robbed a second time. Another precaution was that of putting the storeroom outside the building proper, in what was formerly the old manufactory. This was to guard against unforeseen accidents such as fire, and a stock usually averaging some 20,000 boxes was kept in hand. Once, a fire did actually break out, but was speedily doused before it could do real damage.

Staff, in the new factory, wore white overalls, pastry cook hats in the grinding room, and besides manual helps and clerks, included four shorthand writers, and a fleet of travellers. Soon journalists were getting wind of the new pillery. For sheer taste nothing like it had ever been erected in the town. It was not even *aggressively* different, its red brick façade harmonizing naturally with surrounding dwellings. Explored, discussed, praised, no building was ever to be so extensively written up in the local press until 1964 when the Pilkington headquarters, with their "lake" and magnificent canteen block, were opened in Prescot Road.

When the factory was nearing completion in 1886 *The Building News* printed a picture of it. Rather tactlessly *The British Journal* commented: "Even the writer of a guide to St. Helens could not, without exaggeration, ascribe to the town either architectural or picturesque beauty, and it seems a pity that an erection which would grace the metropolis should practically be thrown away." In the same article Thomas was described as the largest manufacturer of patent medicines in the world. He had developed an industry of "almost inconceivable magnitude . . . through indomitable perseverance".

After such prolonged struggling, eulogies were sweet indeed! Reporters, of course, were encouraged to visit the firm, because of the free advertising this afforded, the kind the Beechams always liked best. For the same reason children potential future buyers were never turned away from the entrance hall, or allowed to leave without clasping some form of advertisement or other.

In 1890 when the quarterly meeting of the Liverpool district of the Institute of Journalists took place, Joseph agreed to a request for forty of them to view the factory. This trip was reported at length in both the *Advertiser* and the *Lantern*. The former waxed especially eloquent over the hall. Here a commissionaire, usually an ex-army sergeant, was in charge, and the visitor made his identity known to him. "If he wishes to see Mr. Thomas Beecham, or Mr. Joseph Beecham, he fills up a form containing his name and nature of business, but commercial transactions are completed by the manager, Mr. Charles Rowed. The attendant, before conveying any message, provides the visitor with the morning papers, views of celebrities, and afterwards invites him to test his solidity on an automatic weighing machine. The visitor is then supplied with a ticket showing his weight and date to remind him of his visit to Beecham's."

Excellent publicity, and a far cry indeed from the cottage/ workshop, where anyone testing his weight during working hours would have been booted into the street.

He, the visitor, was then conducted to a comfortably fitted waiting room, adjoining Joseph's private office. "System reigns supreme!" marvelled the *Lantern*. Two years later the *London Miscellany* expressed its opinion that the place was more "like a palace than a factory". Whilst "Beecham's pilleries", declared the *Town Crier* in 1894, "constitute one of the most handsome structures in town". Brockbank, the writer who had credited a Mrs. Butler with sponsoring the slogan, praised it in his history of St. Helens. The building was the finest and most imposing the town possessed, and would long remain "a monument of the indomitable energy and perseverance, shrewdness and foresight of its owner". *Perseverance*. The word was to crop up again and again in articles dedicated to Thomas's achievements.

In the early 'nineties Beecham's brought out an advertising pamphlet. Entitled *A Familiar Name* it was a purported account of a visit to the firm by a Member of Parliament, and since it is obviously written from the inside is worth quoting in part, as it gives an accurate, though curiously light-hearted, description of the factory as it then was.

His first feeling, the fictional M.P. confessed, was one of astonishment as "my host's coachman drew up at the handsome arched doorway of a stately building with the remark that this was " 'Mr. Beecham's place'." Even after all he'd heard he was unprepared for the splendours of the lofty, three-storied edifice.

The massive glass doors flung open by the burly commissionaire, the treasures of the hall inspected, he was escorted over a delicately blue Persian carpet to the first floor.

On the ledge of a wide window was the visitors' book which

contained the names of many who had "come on a pilgrimage
to this Mecca of globules". Turning sharply to the left the M.P.
was ushered into a visiting room, elaborately furnished in walnut. After being allowed sufficient time in which to examine the
drawings of advertisements plastering the walls, he was shown
in "to the presence of Mr. Joseph Beecham . . . the guiding spirit
of the concern". Chatting to him the M.P. noted that the "same
taste pervaded this, as other rooms. . . . The massive walnut furniture [a wood Joseph obviously favoured], handsome fireplace and
beautiful fittings seemed more worthy of a private mansion than
a business office". It was in this room that the concerns of the
firm were planned. The branches which now extended
". . . throughout the United Kingdom, Australia, India, America,
Canada, the Continent and the East, are all governed by this
quiet, unassuming gentleman as he sits among his carved-wood
figures, Italian marble busts and bronzes in a room which, but
for a pile of letters before him, and the speaking tubes and electric bells at his side, gives no sign of being the head of an extensive business.

"'I had expected to see a much older man than yourself,'
said the M.P.

"'You would have seen one if my father had been here,' the
unassuming gentleman replied, 'but he is taking a well-earned
rest in his home in Buckinghamshire'."

After having been questioned about the advertising (to be related in the next chapter) Joseph escorted his guest to the counting house, where ". . . a dozen clerks were busily engaged to the
accompaniment of the click and rattle of typewriters", and from
there to the works above. Up a short flight of steps and through a
door, which noiselessly closed behind them, the quiet of the
counting house being exchanged for the noise and bustle of
manufactory.

"'Let us commence here in the engine room'," (said the guide).
"'We get the power which drives our machinery from a 12
horsepower gas engine'."

"'And does it require that buzzing demon to make a little
pill?'"

"'I presume,' said Mr. Beecham, 'we might contrive to
make one pill without it, but when one is increased by the
remainder of those we turn out, we could scarcely manage without it.'"

From the engine-room M.P. and guide turned into the room
". . . in which the secrets of the establishment are kept; the
masonic or mixing room". (In this the fictional M.P. was luckier

than real-life journalists, whisked past it.) Through the grinding room, to the making room where pills were being cut into proper shapes at the rate of 15,000 a minute; to the department where eight and a half tons of pills were being dried out.

Enquired the goggling M.P. " 'How many pills does that make?' "

Mr. Beecham did not know, but he pointed out that there were 85 dozen in every stone. On lightning reckoning the M.P. found "that there were no fewer than seventy-seven million, six hundred and eighty-four thousand, two hundred pills being got ready for shipment". And the machines were still in full blast, with twenty to thirty boys belting them out.

The packing rooms were reached, where the boxes were labelled, the government stamp affixed.

" 'I suppose they cost you a good many pounds in the course of a year?' " the M.P. asked.

They did. The regular order was then £600 a week. The previous year (1890) purchases from the government reached £32,000, this, though the law did not compel the use of a stamp when the pills were consigned to agents abroad.

(For 1895-6 the total amount of revenue derived from Medicine Stamp Duties throughout the country amounted to £238,946. If Beecham purchases were still an annual £32,000, and they were probably higher, their own contribution to the revenue amounted to 13½ per cent!).

Next to be inspected was the printing office. Here the presses ran all day. A quick glance into the carpenter and joiners' shop where cases were made for shipment of pills overseas, plus thousands of signs on which advertisements were placed.

" 'Wonderful! " quipped the M.P. " 'I shall begin to respect the pill after today'."

" 'You might do worse,' was the placid reply given with an air of honest conviction that was sledge-hammer like."

From the advertising room the M.P. was conducted into the newspaper room, filled with a series of pigeon holes. "In each compartment is kept a file of the thousands of papers here received, and I fancy that outside the British Museum no such collection of newspapers exists in the world. It may be safely said that any newspaper of any importance published in the U.K. may here be found. Many of the provincial Colonial papers, the leading continental journals, Indian papers galore, hundreds of American organs representing every shade of politics, as well as the society papers which are so numerous in the United States

H

All these were so systematically arranged that any paper could be found in a moment, and any information that was required relative to the advertisement may be found to verify the entry of it made in the ledger.''

M.P. " 'In addition to this record, you enter daily, or weekly, all those particulars, I suppose?' "

J.B. " 'All of them. We can tell all of the particulars without referring to the papers, except in the event of any dispute arising between the accounts sent to us and our books. We have thus a double check, you see, on all our papers'.''

M.P. " 'And these papers are gone through as fast as they come in?' "

J.B. " 'All of them. The advertisement is measured and checked with the order, the credit given the paper for a space occupied by me'.''

The M.P. confessing that he " 'had never seen business conducted in so complete and systematic a manner','' Joseph significantly replied: " 'Well, you see, everything is the result of many years of experience. We are never satisfied to leave things as they are. Whenever we see a chance of improvement we avail ourselves of it and give it a fair and practical trial. It may seem a small thing to make a pill. Perhaps it is, but it requires energy and push to sell it at a profit. In doing the latter we quickly perceived that time was money, and to do everything in the least possible time is what we are always aiming at. Hence it came about that we introduced a system in carrying out all our plans, and I am confident that without that we never could have succeeded'.''

Some of the above amenities, and many of the press tributes, were still in the future, when the premises were opened towards the end of 1887. Early that November a rearing dinner for a hundred of the workmen employed, was held at the Royal Raven Hotel. In the chair, and supported by Charles Rowed, was Joseph. Also present were Walter Andrews, the contractors Messrs. Harrison and Son; engineers J. Heston and Sons; Messrs. Turton and Allen, and the architects, Messrs. Kendow and May, and Mr. Thompson, of Liverpool.

After the removal of the cloths Andrews praised Joseph in a brief speech, in reply to which Joseph stated himself "perfectly satisfied" as to the building by what had been said by gentlemen who had come from a distance to view. He was also, and being at rock bottom non-provincial, "more especially pleased with the remarks by the gentlemen from London who were capable of passing judgment upon the work. They all expressed themselves to the effect that it was impossible to have a better building, and of this he was very proud".

Later, Harrison, the contractor, in his speech, devoutly hoped that "it would be the will of the great architect of the universe that the building should be completed without any accident". A prayer which was answered, since none occurred.

Printing details of this dinner, the *Prescot Recorder* also quoted in full the article from the *British Journal of Commerce* already alluded to.

Thomas, enjoying his well-earned, albeit commuter's rest, stayed away from the proceedings. He disliked public functions in which he might be personally expected to participate. In any case, the factory was Joseph's brain-child, and he was happy to bask in reflected glory. Success had always been inclined to dull the palate, and for him the real excitement, once he had accepted a factory must be erected, had been in the building of the first one. Or before that to the cottage/workshop in Westfield Street. To watching the gross amounts fantastically swell in the green order book. Whilst perhaps nothing, in retrospect, would ever seem such fun as the Milk Street days, where the magic slogan had been coined, where he had indulged in his first advertising copy, and where he had made a friend of adversity. As the Lancashire saying went, "He had all his chairs in the house". He had started the whole thing, and the decade after settling in St. Helens would remain as sharply divided from everything which came later as oil from water, or the peddling years from those spent in Wigan.

Thomas could never be accused of maudlin sentimentality. Towards the slabs of the past he had enjoyed, in the rare moments when he recalled them, he displayed gusty relish. Nonetheless, nostalgia for them could be as acute as it had been when accosting the Cropredy carrier. Or as it was to a correspondent writing to a St. Helens newspaper in 1927, after nearly seventy years exile in America. In imagination this man had gone "along Church-street, by the old post office, and passing the butcher's shop at the corner of Hall Lane, saw the unusually large pig hanging as a Christmas exhibition". He noticed "the stationery shop and stamps office of Mr. Sharp, facing the square and Market-street". Ahead were the offices of the *St. Helens Intelligencer* in whose columns Thomas had first advertised. The writer went as far as "Hardshaw-street, and turned left into New Market Square, and the Market Hall . . . looked into Mr. Pendlebury's pawn-shop. . .", and continued past "Mr. Hulme's bookshop, and so to

Baldwin-street . . . past Dr. Lundell's residence . . . Griffin's photo
gallery . . . and travelled up Combshop Brow . . . coming along
Westfield-street to Arthur-street and Waterloo-street . . . I saw
the Wesleyan School, and in Milk-street cul-de-sac I went to
Beecham's house and again purchased some pills for my father
who was sick".

How great would have been this correspondent's shock had he
returned to the town and attempted to buy further pennyworths
from Beecham's!

More quietly 1887 also saw the close of another era for
Thomas. This was the death on 30th September, and a week before the rearing dinner, of his mother at Curbridge. Granny
Morris was in her eighty-seventh year, had been in extreme discomfort for several weeks, and for two days before she died had
been almost paralysed.

Hastening to Witney, Thomas stayed at an hotel there, from
which he superintended the funeral arrangements. Dignified and
impressive they included a horse-drawn hearse. A further mark
of esteem was the fact that the Rector of Witney, W. Foxley
Norris, officiated, instead of a curate, as would ordinarily have
been the case with a humble cottager. Since Thomas himself believed that burials should be effected as unfussily as possible, the
pomp was probably laid on for the benefit of the clan, who would
have expected a display. As the horses, their black plumes
rhythmically nodding, drew the coffin along the short journey
from the grey stone dwelling to the small church, the spectacle
was so unusual that people rushed to their windows to stare.
Years later the funeral was still being discussed, stored up in
memory, like fat in a camel's hump.

Despite all this, and with his customary abruptness, Thomas
hurried away immediately it was over. In his flight he neglected
to leave instructions for the erection of a headstone, and so none
was ever put up. "Here's fifty pounds for you each," he is supposed to have told his numerous southern relations. "You'll
never see me no more." To his way of thinking there was nothing churlish about this. For almost as long as he had worked he
had succoured the clan, and their children's children. As their
head it had been both his prerogative and pleasure. But they
were all now more or less on their feet, and those that were not
could "look to their own sweat". However, he was to modify
his pronouncement, for he *did* see a few of these relations again,
whom he was incapable of ever visiting empty-handed. There
were also airy promises of bequests he would make at the time

of his own death, particularly to sister Jane. But Thomas must
have had another change of heart, for these were not fulfilled.
His will, singularly brief and uncomplicated for a wealthy man,
was to be contained in four folios of less than 300 words. Apart
from a gift of £100 to his solicitor, and life annuities only of £52
each to his brothers, Thomas left the whole of his property
equally between his sons Joseph and William.

Now all of them, grandparents, parents, aunts, uncles, sisters
and brothers, had died, or left the village. Only the half-sisters,
Fanny and Elizabeth remained in Curbridge. Somehow Granny
Morris's second family had seemed an entirely different breed
from the Beechams. Less voluble, less alive, they were also less
interesting. Though they lived opposite each other the two half-
sisters carried on a deadly feud between them, and were never
seen to converse together. Like many eccentrics, Thomas could
be intolerant of quirks in his fellow ones. Ungregarious and
vinegary, Fanny and Elizabeth were certainly no incentive to
return to Curbridge, and after his mother's death he almost never
went back.

## 13

# AN ORGY OF ADVERTISING

IN 1889 Thomas gave Joseph a half share of the business. It was
none too soon. To all intents and purposes, and for ten years,
his son had been in control.

There was to be no resting on newly formed laurels. "My
father," Joseph remarked of this period, "thought he had reached
the acme, but I knew better, and put my back into it." Again:
"There is no such thing as ill-luck. The man or woman who is
always unlucky generally is so because he, or she, does not grasp
the chance when it comes. Luck is wholly a matter of making
the most of our opportunities."

Putting his back into it, taking the tide of affairs at full flood,
meant expanding overseas trade. By now every Australian newspaper of note carried advertisements for the pills. Insufficient!

The Far East must be assiduously courted, Canada tempted, America stampeded.

Battle with the United States had commenced the previous year by the acquisition of offices in Brooklyn, New York. Part of some premises owned by Pears Soap Company they were, at first, in the nature of a warehouse. Conquest of America was Joseph's biggest gamble, and achievement.

" 'Pardon me'," the pamphlet M.P. had observed during his tour of the factory, " 'but I cannot comprehend your attempting to gain a footing in America, the land of patent medicine and the home of the pill'."

To which Joseph had made lofty answer : " 'We take the broad ground that our pill is the best in the market, and feeling that as we had capital to bring it to the attention of the public, were content to await results'."

These came in replies to seven thousand letters dispatched in the summer of 1888 to chemists in both the United States and Canada. A further three thousand were to follow. Artillery launched, it was supported by the dispatch of a quarter of a million cabinet photographs of the rival candidates for the American Presidency for sale at a low price, the backs of which bore advertisements for the pills. Additional ammunition included 50,000 showcards, and a hundred large cases of medicine.

So much for whipping up American imagination. American palates had yet to be tickled. Unlike the spartan English, and preferring their pills sugar-coated, they got them sweet. Since American packing cases were far superior to English ones, the lids and boxes perfectly fitting, American cases were sent direct to Beecham's from New England. No detail, however trivial, was ignored. " 'It would be a folly to say,' " Joseph told the M.P., " 'that we had no struggle to gain a foothold in that country, but it was all the more gratifying that we did so. Now our business there is so active (approximately only two years later !) and orders are so rapidly increasing, that we have been compelled to put in machinery over there so as to be prepared to meet the rapidly augmenting business, should we be unable to do so promptly from this side of the Atlantic'."

As meticulous, and therefore as successful, was the attention devoted to India. Working on the principle that an army moves on its stomach, 100,000 handbills were distributed amongst soldiers there. Signs and advertising matter were always printed in the language of the country for which they were destined. Not content with this the head traveller was busy learning Hindustani, prior to a tour of India. More than a potential

linguist, Edward Glover was a shining example of Beecham
ability to pick talent. Six feet tall, broad-shouldered, and com-
manding of presence, he was a born actor. Frequently mistaken
for a famous politician it sometimes amused him to encourage
the error. Though modest by nature, where work was involved
he could be flamboyance incarnate. Back in England after an
important tour he would create pandemonium on railway
stations. Arms flaying the air, voice aggressively pitched, he
invariably "lost" a piece of luggage. While porters rushed round
in a frenzied search, Glover artlessly drew attention to the trunks
piled knee-high about him, all thickly bespattered with Beecham
labels. Presently Oldham would drive up in his crisp uniform.
More fuss, drama, noise. By the time Glover decided the moment
had arrived when the missing case could be found, and had
driven off, everyone knew where he had been, and who employed him. An excellent after-dinner speaker, as uninhibited
as Joseph was shy, he accompanied his master on all his travels.
And he had Joseph's thoroughness. Before going abroad he
always made a detailed inspection of the equipment to be taken,
and learnt as much as possible about the country for which he
was destined. "I never like to speak of anything I don't know,"
he averred. When only forty-two he died of pneumonia, an irre-
parable loss to the firm.

It was now, and at long last, that Joseph was able to dig his
teeth into advertising, the medium which had for so many
years been teasing his imagination. The time was ripe for inno-
vation. Manufacturers had ceased to consider it vulgar to advertise. Editors, also, had moderated their prejudices, were eager to
accept all the matter which came their way. In a fast expanding
commercial age the public wanted to be informed about new
commodities and inventions flooding the market. To be told about
condensed milk, typewriters, sewing machines, bicycles, and
portable cameras. The need, both to enlighten, and ensnare, customers, had created a fresh breed of journalist, the professional
agent. Competition was keen, not only amongst manufacturers
with similar articles, but with advertisers themselves, to produce
the most audacious, the most talked-about, the liveliest copy.
And so, week by week, even diehard newspaper proprietors were
relenting. Typographical pattern making went by the board;
display advertisements were accepted in leading newspapers, and
even thumbnail illustrations. The 'eighties saw pictorial art
flourishing in illustrated magazines. A decade later a writer in
*Nineteenth Century* observed that: "Today, *The Times* itself is
ready, subject to certain conditions, to clothe advertisements

in type which three years ago would have been considered fit only for the street hoardings, while even that once intolerable monstrosity, the picture-block, is now cheerfully accepted by journals of the highest standing to emphasize a full-page advertisement."

On the subject of full page advertising Joseph claimed to lead the vanguard in the country. In April 1885 he took a whole page in the *Advertiser*. This was the year in which he launched an advertising campaign which, for scope and ingenuity, was unprecedented in the United Kingdom. As always, facts and figures were to tell their own story. In 1884 Beecham's were advertising in 1,200-1,400 newspapers in Great Britain, and spending approximately £22,000 on the medium. By 1889 Joseph lavished a cool £95,000 a year, raising the sum, two years later to £120,000. After that the amount expended was anyone's guess.

It paid off. In 1899 the *Chemist and Druggist* reported that a Dundee firm had no less an amount invoiced to them than £1,049, whilst of this quantity £719 worth (of pills) had been sent in March. Thomas, in a letter, stated that "such a demand as that experienced by me for Beecham's Pills the last few weeks is unquestionably without parallel in the history of the patent medicine trade. My employees and machinery are working at the highest pressure, and during the last two weeks I have dispatched nearly four tons of pills—net weight!" By 1890 6,000,000 boxes were being sold annually.

Following up the full page in the *Advertiser* fifty more whole pages were taken the same year in top Christmas annuals, including the *Illustrated London News*, *Pictorial World*, and the *Graphic*. Another scoop was affected. The proprietor of an American patent medicine known as St. Joseph's Oil, issued a Book Calendar, two million of which were being distributed free in Great Britain. The only advertisement admitted in its pages— Beecham's Pills. For this insertion a thousand pounds was paid.

In this new, exciting, crazy age of advertising, the sky had become the limit. The race was on, and Joseph having made an impressive start, stepped up his pace, matched skill with cunning, cunning with originality, and romped home an easy winner.

It was an era of gimmicks, stunts, and outdoor signs. Though he forebore to advertise on the Pyramids, and left Nelson's column strictly to the pigeons and other competitors, Joseph made sure that no county, few countries, and if possible, no railway lines, were kept in ignorance of his wares.

Beecham's largest hoarding was along the railway track out-side St. Helens. Eighty by thirty feet, people approaching the town were invited to peer the other side. On doing so they found themselves advised to try. . . . Cottages provided marvellous surfaces for proclaiming the value of the pills, nearly forty in Liverpool alone being used. Cows, in the south, shaded them-selves under Beecham boards. Since people tended to congregate at the seaside in large numbers, seaside towns were a focal point of attack. Bathing vans, often as many as fifty rows deep, were plastered with *the* slogan. In summer steam launches ran up and down popular rivers, including the Liffey in Ireland, where hulls, and every available inch out of water was covered in advertis-ing matter. Indigenous fishermen could apply to the firm for free sails, providing, of course, that advertisements for the pills were painted on them. They wrote in by the shoals, foreign as well as British. "There are yachts," noted the *Town Crier*, "whose sails bear the legend of Beecham's Pills in Australian harbours, donkey carts at watering places setting forth their value, curious craft on Indian seas, all bearing information re-flecting the blessedness of 'Beecham's'." Chemists' shops by the blue Caribbean were ablaze with their virtues. No space was too huge for advertising; none too small, either. Inveigled were London street pianos; and the gummed sides of New Zealand stamps. The latter stunt was also attempted by Sunlight Soap, and proved a flop, though only, according to the president of a New York sales promotion agency, because of antiquated printing methods. Thomas Barratt of Pears Soap was eager to adopt the idea, but the government declined the enormous sum he offered. They re-fused another—to print all the 1891 census forms for nothing, provided Pears Soap appeared on the backs. Angling clubs sent to the firm for "trustworthy (advertising) measures, easily placed in the ticket pocket". They came gratis. And chemists could, and did, apply in increasing numbers for printed advertising matter dispatched by the tons, parcels delivered by rail, carriage paid. Photographs of celebrated actresses, puzzles, story books, and calendars poured from the factory like molten lava.

The "Pretty Girl" had arrived. She had come to stay, and was seen everywhere, riding nude on broomsticks (permissible, since strangely labelled the "spirit of purity"). She exposed an over-sized bosom and wasp waist in elastic textured corsets, brushed her locks in revealing negligées, held, though didn't light, a cigarette. Beecham's used her, though with surprising discretion. Beseeching a railway porter to help her find the box of pills she had brought away from Crewe. Or as Winsome

Wisdom, alias Beauty, a fichu modestly adorning her bosom, listening to Health disclose the all important secret that would help her retain attraction:

A charming young lady I sing in my rhymes,
She's pleasant, good, natural and gracious, sometimes,
Her figure is good, and the glance of her eyes
Will tell you at once she's handsome and wise.

No wonder, since she took. . . .
Topicality was the rage.
Charles Dickens' novel, *Dombey and Son,* was enthralling thousands of readers. Tramping the seashore with his sister Florence, young Paul Dombey learnt that the wild waves whispered to him, not that he would soon be reunited with his dead mother, but that he should try Beecham's Pills. Apropos of this, an astute traveller on his rounds came across a plaster of Paul and Florence cast by the sculptor J. K. Raemaker. Joseph promptly commandeered it, adding it to his parlour/hall collection.

Then Prime Minister, Gladstone carried a Home Rule *Pill* box. Henry Irving's sombre features stared out of magazines as he deliberated whether to Beecham, or not to Beecham. Flattered by this advertisement Irving liked to repeat the story of how, when in Dorset, he had noticed a small girl staring at him. Preening, he asked her if she had ever seen him before. "Oh, yes!" she smiled, "you're one of Beecham's Pills." When an agitation against seven-day newspapers was in full swing, a Beecham advertisement pertinently declared: "All persons who are opposed to the issue of Sunday editions of daily papers, and others who desire to have a quiet, peaceful Sabbath, are invited to throw off week-a-day strain and worry by a timely dose of Beecham's Pills. There is no Sunday labour connected with the manufacture of Beecham's Pills, but they are often to be distributed by chemists on the Day of Rest." Regrettable, though since a box should be constantly kept in the home for use if necessary late on Saturday night in order to ensure a happy Sabbath.

Breaking loose from Barnum's Circus, an elephant raided a Warrington store for jam and onions. No doubt when it reached Beecham's, quipped the *Pall Mall Gazette,* any ill effects would be speedily counteracted. Almost within hours of reading this a pictorial advertisement was brought out by the firm showing the elephant doing just this. In a heavy storm at Blackpool, Nelson's battleship, *Foudroyant,* jerked from its moorings, partially capsizing. An agent from the firm rowed out, draped the hull with advertising matter. For such daring Beecham's were obliged to pay substantial damages, but the furore evoked was worth it. They again capitalized on events at Southsea, when a rowing boat overturned. A yacht with advertising sails providently happened to be near, inspiring a drawing of a boat with the *double entendre*, "Beecham's to the Rescue".

Perhaps the cleverest of all the topical advertisements assumed the form of an open letter to Tanqueray when the play was staged in London:

> Dear Tanqueray, [it ran]
> We venture to think that many of the complications which have arisen during the latter period of your existence, might have been altogether obviated if you and your family had acted upon the advice we have for years been offering. We are led to believe that the necessity for a second Mrs. Tanqueray arose from the fact of the decease of the first Mrs. Tanqueray, this being so we assert that had you insisted upon a judicious use of Beecham's Pills by the first Mrs. Tanqueray, her sphere of life might have been extended to the present time, and you would have been saved from many complications.

Testimonials were still used, and continued to provide welcome free advertising. On 12th July, 1894, the *Windward* left Greenhithe sailing to Franz Josef Land with an expeditionary force. Nothing was heard of it for fourteen months, and it was given up for lost. Hardship was extreme. Two sailors died, and others sustained severe frostbite. But not the ship's carpenter, who wrote to Thomas that he was one of the very few members of the crew who had suffered no ill effects on "one of the most perilous Arctic voyages ever recorded. I did not have one day's illness, and I took no medicine but 'Beecham's Pills'." Supplied to the Expedition, also, and its only dentifrice, was Beecham's Tooth Paste. This commodity, which the firm had recently started manufacturing, was prepared at the New York Depot. For some reason it never caught on, and was eventually discarded.

Humour, as in contrast with the more serious type of advertising in Thomas's day, was "in". Neither Thomas nor his contemporaries could ever have even gently mocked their own products, as did the M.P. in *A Familiar Name* when he enquired if the buzzing demon of the gas engine was required to make a little pill, and vowed to respect it in future. Cyclists whizzed round hairpin bends, every ill was dangerous. Pelicans, parrots, men in nightgowns, found themselves unable to rest until they had taken their daily or nightly stint of medicine. In a rare "near" advertisement a witness, squinting through a keyhole, had been upset to see the respondent and correspondent banding a box of pills about. "Then he was, after all, only her Guide, Pill offerer, and Friend," Counsel, looking remarkably like Joseph, affirmed.

Universally accepted, advertising was considered sufficiently respectable for Royalty to appear in testimonials. Queen Victoria sipped Cadbury's Cocoa in railway carriages. She also busied herself at a desk in a Beecham advertisement which prudently included a labourer's home, the inference being that the pills were as welcome in the palace as the cottage.

Curiously, in an age of stunts, Beecham's recoiled from the more daring ones. Joseph's finger remaining firmly pressed to the public pulse, he was always quick to retreat when this leapt unduly. The pills, therefore, were not heralded on cliffs, advertising matter did not blot out the skies, was not ejected from guns. A risky trick, however, for which Thomas was responsible, was the famous incident of the hymn books. Myth makers have argued over it subsequently, but it seems that about this time a correspondent to the *Hull Examiner* wrote in that a certain impecunious Church of England congregation at South Sheilds found themselves hard up for hymnals. Put to the vicar that he might obviate expenses if he could get an advertisement of a harmless character inserted into a new stock, he approached Beecham's. Suave assent. In due course a supply of books was dispatched. Puzzled to find no advertisement between the pages, the vicar concluded that Thomas had generously made him a present of the hymn books. Until a black Sunday just before Christmas when the congregation inadvertently found itself singing:

> Hark! The herald angels sing
> Beecham's pills are just the thing
> For easing pain and mothers mild,
> Two for adults one for a child.

Thomas hotly denied the story. Not only was it baseless, but no-one with much sense would have been taken in by such nonsense! The verse, he insisted, had appeared originally in a slightly different shape in one of the firm's postcard competitions several years earlier. Correct, or otherwise, pedlars were nevertheless hired to hum it up and down the country, whilst children chanted it through the streets of St. Helens.

In newspaper and illustrated advertising, in printed matter, hoardings and suchlike, Beecham's moved, with, and sometimes nearly always a jump ahead of the times. But in four ventures they were absolutely unique.

A slim brown booklet, entitled Beecham's Help to Scholars, made its bow in 1899. Dispatched, on request, to schoolmasters, it soon became a standard work, and was especially useful to poor children. Data was comprehensive, and included geographical definitions, foreign words and phrases, and an international table of atomic weights of the chemical elements. By the first year four million had been sent out, by 1927 thirty-seven million; and by 1959, a surprising date still to be issuing it, some forty-seven and a quarter million had been distributed!

Almost as popular were Beecham's Views, photo-folios, containing twenty-four views of various towns or regions, retailed at 2d. each—five cents in the States. "Beautifully executed . . . they sell beautifully," commented the *Book News Trade*. Even more ecstatic was the *Boston Republic*. Many a man had found a lump rise in his throat as some picture in one of these neat little books had presented to his mind some scene of his childhood with startling vividness.

Beecham's Oracles were particularly ingenious. Ostensibly plain pieces of paper on which, when ignited, could be descried famous faces such as the Prince of Wales, or the Marquis of Salisbury, and forty million of which had been dispatched within a few years of their inception on request to schools and the trade.

And for an age which made most of its amusements round its home fires over twenty volumes of music folios were brought out. Each one contained thirty different songs complete with original symphonic and pianoforte accompaniments in full. Priced at a moderate 1s. 6d. in cloth, 2s. limp leather, post paid, they actually found favour with *The Times*, which deemed them "an admirable deviation from the more prosaic paths the proprietor treads". Gems abounded to suit all tastes, all nationalities. Thus, "Th' Little Sawt Lad" rubbed shoulders with "Edelweiss". "The Washington Post", "The march from Tanhauser", competed with "Cherry Lips", the "Canadian Boat Song", "Loch Lomond". "Men of Harlech", "The Emerald Isle", and "The Good Rhein Wine", were all there. A must was "What are the Wild Waves Saying?" and there was, there had to be, "A Guinea a Box Polka". As with the three other items these music folios were enormously popular.

The scope and cleverness of Beecham advertising titillated the press, as well as the public. Seriously commented upon, it was frequently compared, invariably to its advantage, with the advertising copy of other patent medicine rivals. The *American Illustrator* was to find that whereas Holloway spent incalculable sums on the medium, his methods were anything but scientific. Seldom varying, his copy was hammered home day to day, week to weeek, month to month. Conversely, Beecham advertisements displayed originality, whilst some of the pictorial ones were "artistic productions of a high merit".

Who was responsible for the advertising? Beecham's never employed agents in Great Britain, though later Joseph engaged the services of a London firm for his foreign trade. The answer lies in the plural. Invited to submit ideas, the general public eagerly complied. Among the most effective were those sent in by a clergyman. Rowed, a skilled copywriter, had charge of the bulk newspaper advertising. A daughter was an excellent draughtswoman. Instigator of the campaign was Joseph, who unquestioningly supplied the musical slant.

Like Thomas before him, Joseph possessed his mentors. Of these the most influential were Thomas J. Barratt, and (Sir) Thomas Lipton. Both were personal friends. Joseph was to become a director of the Pears Soap Firm in which Barratt was a partner, and he was an ardent admirer of the latter's advertising flair. Barratt's career was positively scintillating. In 1865, when only twenty-four, he had been made a partner in the soap firm. At that time the company's annual advertising bill had been a mere £80. But Barratt thought in far more grandiose terms. "Any fool," he is reputed to have said, "can make soap. It takes a clever man to sell it!" So revolutionary were his ideas, so relentlessly did he pursue them, that within ten years the founder's grandson withdrew from the business whilst any remained. Wisely, however, he retained £4,000 in the firm. Barratt quickly pushed up advertising expenditure to between £100,000 and £130,000. A member of the staff suggesting a catchphrase, much as a customer had prompted Thomas's, Barratt pounced on it. Like greased lightning "Good morning! Have you used Pears Soap?" swept through two continents. Another, "How do you spell soap? Why P-E-A-R-S of course!" Indelibly linked Pears and soap in the public mind. His puzzle posters often kept crowds as many as fifty strong staring at optical illusions in a hypnotic trance. Barratt's most sensational coup was the securing of Millais' painting of Bubbles, the wistful little boy with the curls and clay pipe. Exhibited in full colour in the press, a tablet of his transparent soap was artlessly inserted into the bottom left-hand corner of the picture. £2,200 was paid for the original painting, and a further £20,000 said to have been spent on the first reproductions.

At this period Lipton was just easing into his stride. For him commercial fame began by the driving of fat pigs through the streets of Glasgow under a banner of Lipton's orphans. Now the world was coming to be plastered with his name, Ceylon was his colony, and by 1890 he was cheerfully paying £35,000 customs tax on his teas.

Though advertising had taken such a dramatic turn since Thomas's day ("Judicious advertising pays", he asserted, but Joseph was proving that daring advertising paid much better) Thomas still continued to dabble in it. What actual copy he contributed at this date must be conjectural, but no doubt it amused an old dog to show frisky puppies a trick or two. "Reader—Persevere", users of Beecham's Help to Scholars were enjoined, a command strongly evoking the sentiment on his 1842-3 staff. "Reader. If you will you may succeed in wonderful things."

A knitting sheath Thomas had engraved for a Cropredy girl in 1842 carried the tender message:

> Death has been here and borne away
> A sister from your side
> Just in the morning of her day;
> As young as you she died.

Lines which find an echo in the jingle below, the advertisement of a bride radiantly clutching a bouquet after, of course, having taken a dose of pills.

> A maiden in life's spring-time faint and weak
> And smitten down with fell consumption's hand,
> The hectic flush upon her fair young cheek
> That piteous scourge of this our northern land.

Another couplet in the same advertisement:

> An old man in the winter of his days
> With laboured breath and many a bitter pain. . . .

is also highly reminiscent of Thomas's inverted, lyrical style. Both verses are markedly superior to those extolling Winsome Wisdom's figure.

Thomas's early advertising has been criticized as extravagant, given over to preposterous claims. In fact, exactly the reverse is true. If he affirmed, as he did, that his pills cured disturbed sleep, frightful dreams, and all nervous and trembling sensations, it was because innumerable people in unsolicited testimonials were saying just these things. Professionalism was instinctive, absolute. After settling in St. Helens he quickly shed hyperbole, made less use of capitals, fewer and fewer references to truth, and was, compared to his rivals, extraordinarily moderate in his copy.

Extravagance, when it did erupt, was invariably a weapon used to silence detractors, rather than to win clients. He was never irresponsible, never vulgar. If the kind of letter ever arrived at his house which was received by another medicine proprietor, in which a client, having taken two boxes of the latter's remedy, parted with more than four hundred worms about an inch in length (one actually a yard long!) he, at least, had the good taste not to print such details.

Proof that Thomas's former copy was not out-moded, that it had evergreen sales drive, was evinced by the fact that Joseph and Rowed continued to use much of it virtually unchanged for several more decades. The pills, in 1861, were admitted by thousands to be beneficial, it was no fiction. It was still no fiction in 1899 in a *Liverpool Daily Post* advertisement almost word for word intact as that being printed in many provincial papers as late as 1901. The undeniable fact was that it was forceful, pungent, often quite simply impossible to improve upon.

Vitality, attack, universal appeal, Thomas's copy contained these three essential ingredients. Absurdity and verbosity he eschewed. How lack-lustre are the lines from an advertisement in the *Witney Gazette*, 1916: "Consider how essential it is that so important a function should be maintained unimpaired, and constantly equal to the demands made upon it. While it is generally true that a sound digestion implies good health, it is always true that a weak or impaired digestion means—in greater or lesser degree—a poor state of health," compared to Thomas's, "The proprietor of these pills challenges the whole world to produce a medicine to equal them for removing the above-named complaints, and restoring the patient to sound and lasting health". (*Wigan Observer*, 1872.)

Or that for the cough pills: "As a remedy for asthma, difficulty in breathing, shortness of breath, tightness and oppression of the chest, wheezing, etc. these Pills stand unrivalled . . . they especially remove that sense of oppression and difficulty of breathing which nightly deprive the patient of rest. They give almost instant relief and comfort to those afflicted with the above." (*Almost*, note!)

Today, Beecham's Powders, manufactured after Thomas's death, still give quick relief. Whilst not Joseph, Rowed, or the hundreds of people who submitted ideas, nor the modern advertising agent, have ever been able to better Thomas's original slogan, Worth a Guinea a Box. Probably, in the final analysis, this had more selling power than all the oracles, views, music portfolios, and full-page advertisements put together.

Pill-making room in the Mecca of globules

The factory in pony and trap days

Joseph and Josephine, Thomas Beecham's son and daughter-in-law

And on the subject itself Thomas has had the pithiest statement.

In 1902 *Science Siftings,* in a consumer protection feature, gave "without hesitation" its Certificate of Merit to Mr. Thomas Beecham, of St. Helens, Lancashire. Not only were the ingredients of his pills praised, but they were said to contain nothing which could not be substantiated. The following year *The Doctor* also paid tribute. But before this Thomas had acknowledged his Certificate in a succinct paragraph in *Progressive Advertising.*

"It is possible by plausible advertisements, set forth in an attractive style, to temporarily arrest the attention of a number of readers, and induce them to purchase a particular article. But it is a more difficult matter to ensure their continued patronage. Unless the advertised article proves to be all that is claimed for it, not only do the purchasers discontinue its use, but warn others against it as a thing to be avoided. Should it be, however, of genuine value, those who make a trial of it naturally become habitual users and advocates, their advocacy being the most effective and absolutely reliable advertisement possible."

By the end of the century advertising had reached frenetic proportions. In 1901 the Prince of Wales implored commercial enterprise to wake up if foreign competitors were not to steal their colonial trade. The truth was, firms found they must advertise, not so much to save their country, as to survive. And survive they did, hysterically. Balloons and parachutes filled the air. The white cliffs of Dover were snapped up. Handbills were flung into hansom cabs, railway carriages, restaurants. A new kind of violation was achieved when a Royal Academician, relaxing in his garden, heard a sudden report of artillery. From the sky fell masses of coloured papers advertising a tooth powder. Scattered over two acres they took a week to clear up. Abroad, the pace was even hotter. Advertisements daubed the Thousand Isles of the St. Lawrence; a margarine factory painted slogans on walls as far as the Arctic Circle; in Washington a bureau existed solely for the purpose of supplying unsolicited testimonials.

The result was inevitable. Vaulting ambition, o'er-leaping itself, was given a sharp check. A public which had been enthralled became vexed, then outraged. No longer was Holloway permitted to advertise on the Pyramids. Despite tantalizing offers, Cape Town authorities refused to lease Table Mountain for a hoarding. By-laws restricted the use of flashing electric signs, in any case deemed to be dangerous. In 1890 a soap com-

I

pany was compelled to remove a sky sign from Ludgate Hill which, anticipating the 1960s, concealed St. Paul's Cathedral. Alfred Austin, later Poet Laureate, expressed general disgust in a rather banal verse in which he querulously wanted to know if nothing could be protected from the lust of gain.

> . . . nor grove, nor mead,
> Nor silent Pool, no solitary lane,
> Where tender souls, world-weary, may obtain
> The peace they covet and the rest they need?

Perhaps, unfairly, censure was mainly directed against the presumptions of medicine men. A reason why, earlier on, reputable firms had refused to advertise in newspapers had been because they declined to share the same columns as "quacks". Leading American agencies were still apt to drop their patent medicine accounts immediately they could afford to do so. After 1892 the *Ladies Home Journal* went so far as to refuse to carry medicinal announcements of any kind whatsoever.

Though by no means the worst offenders against good taste, Beecham's, being the largest advertisers, came under heaviest fire. Complaints and retaliations often assumed somewhat childish tactics. At Bowness on Lake Windermere the firm had erected an enormous, gold-lettered metal sign. Local vigilantes tearing it down, threw it into the water. Undaunted, Beecham's responded by purchasing a yacht and advertising on the sails. They had scored, but to make certain, concealed a constable in some nearby bushes. Just as well, for in the early hours of the morning their enemies returned, and drilled a hole in the bottom of the boat. An unpleasant situation was averted by John Ruskin putting in an impassioned plea for the "preservation of unsullied beauty". Rather surprisingly concurring, Rowed tartly observed that "Evidently there are very aesthetic people at Windermere".

Rudyard Kipling was another celebrity who grumbled about the "beplastering of railway platforms with every piece of information in the world except the station". Echoed the *Blackburn Times*: "It has been pointed out that a stranger who is whirled along the interminable tunnels of the Underground Railway in London with a ticket in his pocket for Gower Street or King's Cross . . . is continually staring at the signboards as the train stops, only to find he has arrived at Pear's Soap, Colman's Mustard, or Beecham's Pills." Momentarily forgetting Christianity, General Booth declared that if he was wealthy he would put salvation on the hoardings, and run Beecham's right

out. An ally was found in Mr. W. S. Caine, M.P. who brought
forward an abortive bill to limit advertising in rural places.
Testily, and as if they were the sole miscreants, he explained:
"It's to stamp out Beecham's."

Beecham's had no intention of being stamped out. To Joseph
advertising was both a necessity, and a splendid sport. Ever
obsequious, however, at least on the surface, anxious to soothe
the public, he arranged a dinner in the summer of 1893 at the
Holborn Restaurant, his guests being other manufacturers. The
expressed intention was to discuss the science of advertising. Included in the party were Mr. G. P. Reckitt of Reckitt and Sons,
Ltd.; Mr. R. J. Ward of Scott's Emulsion; Mr. McAdam, Rizine
Food; Mr. Adolph Tuck of Raphael Tuck and Sons; Mr. J. E.
Cockett; Messrs. W. H. Smith and Son, and his crony Thomas
Barratt. Light relief was provided by the Mastersingers, who
gave an "example of the perfection in which part singing can
be brought by a trained body of choristers".

*Punch* was facetious about the proceedings:

> To think of five-score puffers all seated at a table,
> A-puffing one another just as hard as they are able;
> And each one just contriving (with a cunning eye to Pelf)
> Whilst he sings his neighbours' eulogies, to advertise himself),
> What heights of noble courtesy—no common folk could reach 'em,
> When C-rt-r's Little Liver Pills say pleasant things to B-ch-m.

The last line was a dig at Carter's offer to withdraw their rail-
side advertising which so offended the public. Thomas had followed suit, but with reservations. He would, he said, remove his
advertisement from bathing huts at Scarborough, only on condition that no other firm was allowed to advertise there. "While
they are open to be used in this way, the desecration may as
well be Beecham's Pills as any other."

The dinner resolved very little. Joseph put up fewer signs, but
extended advertising in other directions, thus having his cake
and eating it, at which he was adept. But at least the British
public could flatter itself its grumbling had not entirely fallen on
deaf ears. Apparently malefactors existed who believed as fer-
vently as itself that advertising should be an art, and not an
abomination, should be kept within the bounds of decency.

But not Thomas, who had not dined in London, cared nothing
for mastersingers, and to whom criticism was never less than
a gross impertinence. The embryo author in him ached for his
pen, and a speech made by the Prime Minister, Lord Rosebery, at
a Royal Academy dinner, gave him his opportunity. In it Rose-

bery scathingly enquired how the landscape master, Turner, would feel if he were resurrected and could see the vessels he had so gloriously painted turned to pill advertising? For his text he chose a powerful tirade conducted by Jerome K. Jerome in his paper, *Today*, in which desecrators of the countryside were dubbed "Fiends in advertising garb".

Thomas's scalding remarks to Jerome were reprinted that year in the *Dover Express*.

"No-one enjoyed Lord Rosebery's speech more than I did, and if any doubt had previously existed in my mind as to the affectiveness of this form of advertising, he dispelled it. Much has been said of this being an American idea, but boards have been used in fields by my firm for ten years, and by English advertisers in a small way further back, but like all good things it is being spoilt by so many taking it up." This fact alone, Thomas continued, "is sufficient to ensure me it is time to stay my hand and 'look for pastures new', and I would like to suggest to any 'Landscape Spoiler', that if for reasons best known to himself he is wishful to retire from the field, now is an auspicious time to declare his intention. I am fully convinced there is very little interest [taken] in the matter by the general public, and it is to them I call, and if the few who are desirous in keeping 'A Beautiful World' would worry their minds more about the ugliness and squalor of the streets where people have to dwell, they would be better occupied in trying to gratify their present whim, and by so doing depriving farmers, fishermen, and others from getting a little help. There has been a lot of exaggerated rubbish written and spoken as to what advertisers intend doing; they have to exercise their judgement as to what amount to spend on one system; and I question when Ledas wins the Derby if the amount of her gains for her illustrious owner would provide with sails all the boat-owners who have applied to me. I am sorry to have disappointed so many and benefited so few. Again it is against the interest of any advertiser to put up these expensive boards too closely, and my fixers, I am sorry to say, have erred in this respect in some instances, which will have to be rectified as with any 'nice bits of stuff' as a Liverpool lawyer once described a lovely view to me, and this reminds me how differently landscape affects individuals. I was about two years ago having lunch at the head of Lake Coniston and a lady and gentlemen were seated at the same table. I was interested when she remarked to her companion, 'See, my dear, that is the Coniston Old Man,' and his answer, which was brief, bears out my argument, for it ran, 'What, that wretched thing!' "

Evidently Thomas was not always above enjoying a joke against himself. This letter, which, though provocative, appears to have gone unanswered, was also printed in *Health,* and *Science Siftings.*

Opposition to an advertisement Thomas had installed at Holywell, facing St. Winifrede's Well, involved him in another fracas. However, upon the Duke of Westminster's agent writing him that the well was the property of His Grace, he had the board removed. Like Windermere, Holywell appeared filled with singularly aesthetic people, for soon Thomas was declaring that, though he had been offered several other sites in the vicinity, he had decided not to fix boards in the town again, and "public indignation may now rest appeased".

May 1893 found him stoutly defending his bathing hut advertisements at Scarborough. "Indignant" in the *Sheffield Telegraph,* complained that these abominations had driven him from that town to Filey, and that he did not intend returning till Scarborough had done its duty. Backing this up, another correspondent finished his letter with an ominous: "Mr. Beecham will understand me when I conclude with the remark, 'Remember Windermere!'" Thomas's reply to "Indignant's" grouse was in a mood of flippant patronage, ". . . in order to prove the writer at least a dreamer". It was strange, because the Filey bathing vans had been painted with his advertisements well before those at Scarborough. A terrible shock for "Indignant", who would obviously wake up to find himself out of the frying pan into the fire. With a jaundiced glance at Beecham advertising sails this correspondent had dared jest about the souls of brave fishermen. He had better look to his own, Thomas threatened, unless, of course, he was "like unto 'bipeds' who had none. . . . Rest assured the 'old man' will get his for nothing unless he enlarges his mind, but this may not trouble him as there will be no advertising there."

This slightly muddled allusion to paradise was repeated in a letter to *Public Opinion* next year, which again found Thomas defending huts and sign advertisements. "Blots on the beautiful," he promised, "for the sake of monetary gain, will continue to arise long after we four [himself, and three censorious correspondents] have gone to a 'beautiful world', where advertisers cease from worrying, and scribblers are at rest." Shrewdly he pointed out that through his letter to the press he had probably attained the most notable advertisement any firm had acquired, gratis.

A *Beautiful World* was the title of the first number of the

magazine of the Society for the Checking of Abuses in Public
Advertising, founded in 1893. Commented the *Daily Graphic*,
a copy lying on the editorial desk: "No-one can deny that the
present state of English meadows is scandalous." A society which
aimed at putting this down should be zealously supported. Nevertheless the right of a possible Act for making advertising of this
sort illegal must be suspect."It is ever an ill thing tampering
with the people's liberty." Frankly, the *Graphic* doubted whether
any government could touch the matter. Far better to let
S.C.A.P.A. appeal to the advertisers. Not to their sense of pro-
prietory (in which they semed to be grossly lacking) but to their
profit, in which they were not. Let a list be printed of those
vendors of whisky or pills or false teeth who advertised their
wares over English landscapes, and if they persisted in their
attempts let them be boycotted. A conclusion oddly at variance
with the previous remark that personal liberty should not be
assailed.

And there, for the moment, at least so far as Beecham's was
concerned, the pros and cons of outdoor advertising were permitted to rest. Joseph hadn't argued with any newspaper correspondents; Rowed had spoken out once. Perhaps the two men,
with their innate discretion, were able to curb Thomas's spleen.
So long as they kept quiet it was possible to play the publicity
game their own way. Public vituperation could only be damaging to the firm. It might have been in keeping with the old, barn-
style factory. With the magnificent pill palace it was about as
incongruous as a blizzard in July.

# 14

# FATHER AND SON

N o t ten years old, the new factory was running as smoothly
as the old. Hygiene continued to be a fetish, employees scrubbing
floors on Saturday mornings. In summer, when excessive heat
still made pill-making, in large quantities, impracticable, boys
were not laid off, but were kept busy with extra polishing and

dusting. The building, which shone spotless as a hospital, was considered to be every bit as therapeutic as one. "More like a convalescent home in a manner of speaking," a retainer has recalled. The healthy air was said to keep employees immune from colds, just as the townspeople had sworn years ago they had stayed fit simply by inhaling the odours rising from Thomas's backyard shed.

Because of these healing vapours, because of the airy conditions at a period when factories were too often holocausts of dirt and discomfort, because of the amenities offered, there was still, despite the continued modest wages, no difficulty in acquiring staff. Free cocoa and tea were provided, also a billiards table, and a large reading room in the basement for after-dinner relaxation. Additionally, Joseph, who had kicked round cobbled streets as a boy, and knew only too well the need to let off steam in safety, purchased a piece of recreation ground for younger workers close to the printing office. Leisure, which Thomas and his contemporaries had never really known, was, in fact, gradually infiltrating into workers' lives in the town. Reluctant as St. Helens had been to adopt it, half days had been granted to shop assistants (though not always pressed) in 1884. Twelve years before that date a nine-hour day had been grudgingly adopted. In 1890, under Joseph's auspices, the rigid 6 a.m. to 6 p.m. hours at the factory were relaxed, and an eight-hour day introduced, with Saturdays from 9 a.m. to 4 p.m.—for the employees *only*, Joseph himself frequently putting in sixteen hours at his desk, working an 80-84 hours week, to his staff's approximate 50! When he came to be knighted the family motto chosen to accompany the arms, escallops, martlets, and a swan's crest, was, significantly enough, *Nil Sin Labore*.

Paid holidays were still far away, but Beecham's organized an annual outing for their workers. A typical example was that reported by the *Advertiser* in August, 1887. "On Saturday last eighty employees of Messrs. Beecham and Son journied to the Great Eastern Hotel, New Ferry, to hold an annual picnic." The party set out at 6 a.m. At Liverpool they took the steamer to New Ferry; at 8 a.m. sat down to breakfast. At one o'clock healthy north country appetites were satisfied by a weighty dinner. Throughout the day various sports were held, prizes awarded successful competitors. A knife and fork tea was served at 6 p.m. after which dancing went on till dusk, when the homeward journey was commenced, the party returning to St. Helens at midnight.

Beecham's were not alone in giving their staff annual treats.

As far back as 1859 Kurtz Chemical works were holding them, the *Intelligencer* mentioning a Christmas tea party at which a band had played favourite selections. What *was* unique about Beecham's was the gusto of the proceedings. Play was as intense as work. Wagonettes, seaside junketings, three slap-up meals, and all the fun of the fair, were infinitely more dashing than sedate munching to the tunes of palm court orchestras. Everything was always marvellously rounded off, too. When members of the Institute of Journalists had asked to inspect the firm in 1890 they were given lunch afterwards at the Fleece Hotel, which they had not requested. And when they wound up events with a visit to the Earl of Derby's Knowsley Hall seat, Joseph, who was already beginning to complain he lived "a rushing life", nevertheless found time to join them in the stage-coach, revelling in the trip as much as anyone.

So popular, in fact, were these outings, that the employees' sheer enjoyment proved their undoing. Queen Victoria's Diamond Jubilee was celebrated by a week's holiday, passed in the Isle of Man. Married men were allowed to take their wives, and owing to the numbers the trip was arranged in two sections. The venture was repeated at King Edward's coronation. And it was on this occasion that one of the parties, becoming "overly merry", the practice was abruptly discontinued.

Was there no grumbling, no dissension in this Mecca of Mecca's? Yes, once. The firm employed some Polish hands, who, having been turned out of their country as being revolutionary types, began to cause trouble at the works. On learning about it Thomas choked with rage, and thereafter the word "Pole" could never be pronounced in his presence without causing him near apoplexy.

The palatial pill factory had at last given the Beechams social standing in the town. International, as well as national prestige, was accorded them by the mammoth advertising campaign. Thus, with two stones, and for all time, obscurity had been successfully laid. They had arrived, and if Joseph could not publish his pedigree as Messrs. Haddock, Gamble, and Pilkington had recently done, he had at least ensured that Beecham was now one of the foremost families in St. Helens. He was to be heaped with civic honours. Elected to the Town Council in 1889, elected alderman in 1901, Mayor of the Borough three times—1899-1900, and 1910-11-12. Coveted as these accolades were, they proved a mere *hors d'oeuvre* to those which glittered beyond the borders of industrial Lancashire.

An inevitable, and gratifying, result of so much publicity was that the firm now benefited from "free" advertising in ever increasing measure.

> To the country I will go without question,
> Forgetting this world and its ills,
> And to relieve my great indigestion
> Will take some of Beecham's good pills. . . .

went the local pantomime quatrain, to be hummed over the town like the hymn verse distortion.

Jokes and anecdotes abounded. Observed *Tit-Bits*, at Christmas: "The holly with which we decorate our homes would strip a hollywood the size of the New Forest . . . if all the shops in the Strand were owned by chemists, and each shop was stocked by Beecham's Pills, they would scarcely be able to supply the demand for these delicacies after the Yuletide carousel." There were quiz games galore, one from *Scenic Liftings* being a typical example. *Brown*: "Have you a guinea you can lend me?" *Jones*: "No, but I have a. . . ." Seven hundred competitors submitted the correct answer. When a schoolboy was asked what St. Helens was famous for, and replied pills, Thomas was so delighted that he made him a present of a watch. Around the time Richard Pilkington was elected to Parliament, Thomas had some coal delivered to his house. Passing by with a friend a bishop exclaimed, "Ah, there is the result of the election". "Where?" queried his companion. "Why, there," the bishop pointed to the coal sacks, "Can't you see the Pill-King-Tom?" An American tourist, shown round Earl Beauchamp's stately home, and lost in admiration of all he saw, the lawns, deer, splendid mansion, murmured awedly: "This is magnificent! And I suppose it has all been made out of those blessed pills of his?" And yet another from *Punch*. *The Mem Sahib*: "I wonder if you have got such a thing as Lemon Peel and Candied Peel in your shop?" *European shopkeeper*: "No, Mem Sahib. Only got it Cockle Peel and Beecham Peel."

More seriously inclined were the magazines which suggested the pills for remedies which must even have surprised Thomas. *Companion* advised them for the removal of blackheads. A rabbit breeder in *Fur and Feather* noted that his pets did not die off like those of other exhibitors after shows. Bread and milk followed an hour later by a dose of Beecham's pills worked wonders. Correspondents were urged to try them for red eyelids, languor, and in the case of "Working Man's Wife", for an enlarged stomach. This might, of course, have been produced from causes incidental to her age, but as a possibility. . . .

The first indication that a Beecham had "made the grade" locally, was an invitation extended to Joseph and his wife, to attend Mayor Alderman McBryde's At Home in the Town Hall in 1866. An unexciting affair. Quaffing tea, and chewing buns, Joseph had other ideas about mayoral functions, but as with advertising nearly two decades back, was content to keep his opinions to himself, and mark time. Important invitations now began to come thick and fast. Already Joseph was helping to promote a local railway. Inheriting Thomas's love of the theatre he was also bestirring himself on behalf of the Theatre Royal. Originally situated in Milk Street, where the family had first settled, it was moved to Corporation Street. Later, when the building came to be burnt down, and an opera house erected on the site, Joseph was, with Sir David Gamble, and Councillor Dixon Nuttall, among the first directors.

Mixing with the élite, playing a vital rôle in municipal affairs, entailed lavish hospitality. Accordingly, and in the summer of 1885, when the new factory was going up, Joseph had moved to Huyton, the little village six miles away, and which was then surrounded by open countryside. Here, privet hedges were marvellously sweet-smelling, and the air was as fresh and bright as he remembered it long ago at Aunt Jane's.

Joseph's square, cream-painted house, Ewanville, was much more in keeping with his growing eminence than the Westfield Street one. It was also an ideal place in which to entertain. Of its thirteen acres, all but two fields where horses and cows grazed, were cultivated. Visitors, wandering over the shelving lawns, could admire the orderly flower beds, the Muscat grapes, tropical ferns, and exotic orchids reared in the pile of conservatories. Though Oldham drove the pony and trap, and factory brougham, Joseph also employed a Huyton groom. Underwood had been in service with the Earl of Derby, and his beautiful white breeches were the talk of the neighbourhood.

Indoors, Ewanville was a veritable Aladdin's cave, crammed, like the factory, with the many treasures its owner had picked up on his travels. To stroll about and appraise them was a delightful novelty. Pictures of the Bridal Falls and the Grand Canyon, Venetian glass, Crown Derby Jardiners, lacquer bowls, inlaid Chinese mother-of-pearl screens, ivory tusks, French bronzes, and Satsuma ornaments by the dozens were crowded into every square inch. The house was actually centrally heated, whilst

it was also lit by electricity, a private plant said to be the first
to be installed in any home in the country.

If the visitors had sufficient energy left over after a monu-
mental meal, they could take their turn at an eleven foot billiards
table in what was virtually a music room. Here, a two-manual
hand blown organ was later replaced by an electrically blown
one, and against another wall stood a magnificent orchestrion.
Imported from Geneva it was fed by perforated rolls, fresh con-
signments of which arrived every month from Switzerland.
Young Tom, Joseph's son, had been enormously excited when,
"big as the side of a cottage", it arrived at the house. The super
musical box, as he was to write, "performed symphonies of
Mozart and Beethoven, preludes and selections from the operas
of Verdi, Rossini, and Wagner, and miscellaneous pieces of a
dozen other composers great and small". And as the youthful
Walt Whitman learned the making of song from the birds of the
South that sang to him, so Tom, listening daily to the musical
sounds that rolled round his ears "began to comprehend something of the grandeur and pathos, of the fire and tenderness, that
dwelt in the souls of those masters dead and gone".

Perhaps because it was unique this music/billiards room tended
to impress guests more than the drawing-room, which had gar-
lands and tendrils embossed on the ceiling, was richly brocaded
and carpeted, and where the grand piano was covered in bur-
gundy velvet. A cousin of Joseph's, who stayed at Ewanville,
was to recollect it in detail when aged nearly ninety. "It was a
wonderful place. I never saw anything like it. Joseph loved to
play the organ. He'd sit at it for hours. He couldn't sing a note
in tune, but accompanied himself with a kind of croaking hum."
At the same time Joseph's nephew, Edward Pemberton, "might
be playing on a different instrument in another part of the room.
A footman went round spraying the air with eau-de-cologne".

Music, a dominant theme in his home, also crept into Joseph's
working hours. When time permitted, he would improvise on a
piano at the firm, or on the organ which had been left behind
after his transfer to Huyton. This organ was later moved to the
Town Hall for the use of the Parish Church when the latter was
burned down. It must have been an excellent one, for eventually it found its way into St. Andrews Church, where it was
not replaced until 1960.

Joseph's extreme shyness made it difficult for him to unbend.
Though his talents and industry commanded respect amongst
his employees, intimacy was never encouraged, and he was
almost incapable of small talk with them. Only where music,

the great, universal language was concerned, could diffidence break its self-imposed barriers. A worker had merely to be able to play an instrument, to sing moderately well, for Joseph to join him on his bench, and chat effortlessly, regardless of time. One amateur performer was given free tickets to all the musical functions in the town. John Allen, the works engineer, had been persuaded, after considerable inducements, to sell out his interest in Allen and Turton (the factory engineers) and take charge of the complex machinery. The possessor of an exceptionally fine tenor voice he was, to Joseph's chagrin, too old to train. Part of Allen's duties included winding the clock each week. Once ascended to the top of the tower, the impromptu stage, plus the panorama spread out below him, went to his head like wine so that he would burst into passionate song. His voice could be heard half across St. Helens, but the habit was never stopped. An aspiring musician Joseph *was* able to assist, however, was a boy he discovered in a local church choir. At his expense Donald Baylis was sent to Italy to be trained. Eventually he became manager to Tom, when the latter was a celebrated conductor.

Years later the theme of music cropped up again at the firm in an amusing way. This was in 1917, when men were in short supply, and women were engaged for the first time. The welfare officer at the factory selected seventeen girls, "those who had clean finger nails, and, wherever possible piano-playing experience, since agile fingers on the keyboard were expected to be equally agile on the packing line". Joseph would have approved the choice, but not the species. Disbelieving in mixing business with the sexes, whilst he was alive only one female name appeared on the wages list, a married woman engaged in the office. A second reason was guaranteed to make any suffragette see red. Every employee, Joseph considered, when first going to Beecham's should "understand that they could work from the bottom up". Since no woman would ever be put in a managerial position, she started with an impossible handicap.

Despite the pomp and elegance of Ewanville, the outward and visible signs of success, Joseph's appearance still remained homely. "I'm a true cosmopolitan", he once boasted. "My tie I bought in Cairo, my coat in Australia, my boots in San Francisco". Yet he did not look sophisticated, or even bizarre, any more than if he'd have clapped a sombrero on his head he would have looked a cowboy. He resembled a clerk, an assistant, a secretary, anything in fact, but what he was, a wealthy manufacturer. And at the firm he worked with unostentatious thoroughness, never adopting airs, striking attitudes, or playing

the big tycoon. Oldham drove him home each evening, but every
morning he travelled to St. Helens by train so that he could chat
to business friends. Invariably the first to arrive at the factory,
"an old floor-rag of a sheep-dog" (the breed never altered),
bounded at his heels and was tied to a kennel there. A simple
start to a busy day, filled with other endearingly common
touches. Joseph's former home had been incorporated into the
firm, and was used by the commissionaire, the dining-room being
given over to the employees. But Joseph himself did not sit
down to a set meal. A packed hamper was sent over from the
house, and the contents, unwrapped from the snowy white linen
of the north, would be consumed at his desk while he toiled on
and on. When Thomas showed up it was in a frock coat, yellow
with age, which had seen hundreds of mixing sessions.

   Though such opposites in character, father and son had certain
traits in common. Both were gluttons for work, and each was to
give an almost identical answer to reporters concerning the
reasons for success. "Work hard, that is the only way," Joseph
stressed, while Thomas maintained it was perseverance more
than anything else, which had taken him to the top. Both men
liked travelling; had enormous stamina; were excellent mathema-
ticians; methodical in business; pioneers, inventors, and innova-
tors. Neither was easy to get on with, Thomas being too brusque,
Joseph too timid. Both could be merciless, cutting people completely out of their lives when it suited them. By 1896 Walter
Andrews, the works manager, had been with the firm for over
twenty years, had virtually grown up with it, but the axe, when
it fell, struck hard. Returning from lunch one afternoon Andrews
found a poster relating to evening classes at the technical institute pinned up in the hall. Objecting to it he asked Moss, who
was to succeed him, who had put it there. Mr. Joseph Beecham,
apparently. "Then take it down, and give it back to Mr.
Beecham," Andrews foolishly commanded. An utterance which
brought about his swift dismissal. A case in point with Thomas
was his treatment of a work-shy husband of a close relative. For
years Thomas had helped the man, the wife, and her family.
When he finally realized that as long as he continued to put his
hand in his pocket, the husband would go on sponging on him,
aid was promptly and permanently withdrawn. This, though
the children to whom he was devoted, suffered.

   Neither Thomas nor Joseph was snobbish. Thomas, as has been
seen, kept up with old acquaintances. Though Joseph's riches inevitably separated him from erstwhile school friends, when these
were encountered again he was always most courteous. Both men

made unhappy marriages. Both found it difficult to get on with
their own children, and were unfamily-minded, a curiously
Beecham tendency, and one all the more strange in Thomas's
case, since his home circle had been a close one. Neither was
given to confidences, though, as Joseph's son (Sir Thomas
Beecham) was to write: ". . . during the late summer months
and early autumn of 1916", when Joseph died, "he, for the first
time in our association, unburdened himself to me as much as I
believe it was in his nature to do so". An occurrence which was
to have a strange parallel with Joseph's younger son Henry, also
reserved and uncommunicative. Shortly before Henry's own
death he "unburdened" himself to his daughter, talking of his
childhood, which had been unhappy, and oddly reverted to a
Lancashire accent, long since smoothed out.

Both Thomas and Joseph were notorious womanizers, though
according to Joseph's daughter-in-law, Utica Welles, the father
was more subtle than the son. Indeed, Thomas could sometimes
display an old world gallantry. When Utica became engaged to
his grandson Tom, he added, to the expected sovereign, a rose.

Their differences were pronounced. Thomas the complete extrovert, making up his own mind, sticking to it, airing his views
to the world at large, revelling in his eccentricity. Joseph the
awkward introvert, conforming, at least outwardly. Confident
only at work, on other occasions unable to form an opinion without first consulting a clergyman or solicitor. For all his brashness,
the father so cautious in financial dealings; for all his reserve,
Joseph so extraordinarily bold in business. Thomas hot-headed,
violent. Joseph contained, secretive, calm, so ice-cold that no-
one can ever recall his losing his temper. The father's was an in-
tegrated personality, the son's a dual one. Joseph's right hand
seldom knew what his left one was up to. Thomas was unable
to interest Joseph in astrology, or Joseph Thomas in music. Perhaps their dissimilarities were most marked in their attitudes towards the same things. It was Joseph who had turned the business
into a giant organization, who had built the splendid pill factory,
but in time he grew tired of the routine, spending his days increasingly on more artistic pursuits. Pill-making absorbed Thomas
to the very end. Neither man was sentimental, but Thomas, who
had known greater hardship, was affectionate towards the
material milestones of his path, the crooks, staffs and handbills
which had notched it. Though both were dedicated to work, only
Joseph knew the inestimable value of play. Both liked money,
but where Thomas was indifferent to it once earned, Joseph
used most of his to "further the glorious cause of music". Father

and son were philanthropic, but Joseph did not mind if knowledge of his gifts leaked out, since this was publicity for the firm,
and also aided his ambitions. Thomas, on the other hand, would
fly into a rage if details were disclosed. This was partly because
he genuinely preferred to remain an anonymous giver, but also
because he did not want to be touched by undeserving beggars.
Thomas's attempts to enforce secrecy could sometimes be frankly
preposterous, as was the instance when he subscribed to the Congregational Sunday school funds.

He was in the habit of sending the pastor of the Ormskirk
Street Church, then the Reverend J. Ward, bundles of foreign
and other newspapers. Browsing through them one morning,
Ward was astonished to find, scribbled in a margin in Thomas's
unmistakable handwriting, the startling message: "I will give
£1,000 towards your new schools." Afraid it was too good to be
true Ward raced round to Thomas's house, where he was quickly
reassured.

"Will you," barked Thomas, "have it now or later?"

What a dilemma! For Ward, who had no wish to offend his
benefactor, was also acutely aware that a bird in the hand is
worth two in the bush. Clearing his throat he stammered that
he would have *half*—now. Certainly. From a drawer of his roll-
top desk Thomas laconically pulled out five one-hundred pound
notes. These were handed over with the strict injunction that no-
one was to be informed. Ward agreed, though it was natural to
mention the matter to several of the deacons. And still more
natural for one of them to tell his wife. The story was over the
town like wildfire. Ecclesiastical breath was tremblingly held for a
few days, waiting for the blow which never came. Thomas, when
he chose, could be all-forgiving, and £125 was actually added to
the original sum. It is interesting to speculate what would have
happened had Ward omitted to read the marginal note. Was it a
sly joke? Or a test to see whether or not the pastor bothered to
glance at Thomas's advertisements?

(Very different in spirit was this donation from that of an
earlier St. Helens one to an Anglican vicar for *his* schools. Feeling that his donor, a woman, had shown a lamentable degree of
parsimony, the vicar wrote her in no uncertain terms: "You
will pardon me, I trust, for what I am going to say for I must
speak out very plainly. You are beyond question my wealthiest
parishioner and what is the amount I receive from you as your
annual subscription for the support of our schools? Merely five
pounds. . . . If I obtain the land from you, I shall not look for any
further assistance from you for the building fund; if you are still

indisposed to give it, I must tell you that I conceive I have every right to look to you for a subscription of £100: less than this I do not expect from you. . . ." The donor's answer is not recorded, but it would be easy to imagine Thomas's, or Joseph's, in similar circumstances, neither man caring to be taken for granted.

Father and son were also the antithesis of each other in that, whilst both retained accents of speech, Thomas never wished, or attempted, to alter his. On the other hand Joseph's Lancastrian dialect was a perpetual embarrassment to him. Though in time he managed to thin it, it did not disappear. Both were solitary, though Joseph only *consciously* so. Thomas loved company, but could cheerfully dispense with it. Entertaining so lavishly at home, Joseph went out of his way to woo people, yet the cliche of "being alone in a crowd" can seldom have been more appositely applied to anyone. His reticence made it difficult for even his closest friends to understand him well.

Finally, and possibly the greatest difference between the two, was that it was Thomas who was undeniably the younger man. Life never palled. Constantly he courted, sought it out, attacked it, while in due course Joseph found himself running away from his own pattern, searching for remedies to cure unhappiness, and worse—far worse!—boredom.

15

# SOUTHPORT

FOR thirteen years Thomas had been a human pendulum, swinging between Mursley and St. Helens, torn between conflicting loves. Where were his real roots? In his native south, or his adopted north? Indecision was finally resolved in 1892 by the building of a last home at Southport. Stock and furniture at Mursley Hall were sold, and the house eventually given to his grandson Tom, as a wedding present, when the latter married Utica Welles in 1903. Thomas was to pay his chosen county one more priceless compliment, when, in his will, he styled himself "A Lancashire Gentleman".

Ewanville

Wychwood, Southport,
Thomas Beecham's last
home

Joseph Beecham, 1888

Thomas and his sister
Emily, Thomas Beech-
am's grandchildren

Southport, like St. Helens, had developed late, growing out of a craze for sea bathing, a fashion set in 1789 by George III at Weymouth. It was now becoming increasingly popular for business men from Liverpool and Manchester, especially for those who had retired. Thomas chose it for its bracing air, and the fact that it was less than twenty miles from the firm. He may also have been influenced by a sentimental reason, one of his very first orders having been that of a sale to a chemist in Nevill Street there.

A corner site was found just outside the town, and building plans approved by the council on 3rd March, 1892. Today, Norwood Avenue is a spacious, tree-lined road situated between the stations of Hesketh Park and Meol. Over seventy years ago Wychwood was one of the first residences. Double-fronted, composed of plain red brick, and far less pretentious than Mursley Hall, it had a wooden frame porch, and an ample cellar in which Thomas hung his numerous herbs, and stored fruit. At the rear of the sloping garden ran the Yorkshire and Lancashire railway. Spurning his favourite brown paint and varnish, Thomas had the living-room friezes picked out in pretty pastel shades of blue and green. Another colourful touch was a stained glass window at the back of the hall. Wide skirtings and thick mantelpieces were features of the house, every detail of which, as usual, came under Thomas's eagle eye. Some years ago workmen, effecting repairs, were loud in their praises of the building's sound structure. According to its present owner, Mrs. Brooks, much of the decoration and ornamental work has remained unchanged since Thomas's day. Thomas had a good deal of the furniture made at the factory, all of it solid and useful, rather than fanciful.

Taking possession on 31st March, 1893, the souvenirs of seventy-two crowded years were moved into the rooms. Cuttings, photographs, handouts, advertisements, chemical manuals, works on astrology, a scrap book bursting with pressed plants, each one neatly labelled. The pocket, and family bibles; the stick with the hieroglyphic love letter, the staff and crook with their jaunty references to sacred wisdom's ways, and to look up, try again.

Except for the services of a housekeeper, Thomas lived here alone. Five years before his son William had married a solicitor's daughter. He was then thirty-three, his bride, Maud Gladstone Beasley twenty-two, and this time there was no parental opposition. A Beecham was marrying into class, class was uniting with money. William, who had never shown the slightest interest in the factory, qualified as a surgeon in 1885 when thirty years

K

old, his concern for medicine also being minimal. As a boy he had contracted smallpox, Thomas not believing in vaccination, and his face was badly pitted. A laborious conversationalist, he dressed beautifully, wore a top hat whenever possible, and was without humour, "appraising and analysing" every joke made in his presence "with the cool curiosity of a scientist examining a new-found gem under a powerful microscope". William's precision of speech no doubt stemmed from an effort, like his brother, to scrub it free of Lancashire vowels. Like Joseph, too, he was the antithesis of his father, but his disinterest in the pills, coupled with his affectations, made it even more impossible for Thomas to get on with him, and as with his daughter Sarah, Thomas was probably relieved to be permanently rid of William's company.

Thomas still had travel-happy feet. His bits and pieces arranged in Wychwood, he sailed, the same August, to America. The *Chemist and Druggist* noted he intended paying a lengthy visit there. He wanted to "look after the business in New York, visit the giant exhibition at Chicago, and see most of what there is to be seen in North America". A considerable undertaking at more than three score years and ten! Thomas also boasted that he planned to spend several thousands of pounds at the exhibition.

He sailed on the steamship *City of New York*. Also crossing the Atlantic that summer were his grandson, Tom, with Joseph, but on a different ship, the *Campania*. The boy now attended Rossall School at Fleetwood, and Joseph's schedule being even tighter than his father's, Tom returned home alone, helping, though only fourteen, to organize a concert on board ship.

In New York Thomas stayed at a Fifth Avenue hotel, where he gave one of his rare press interviews. "Mr. Beecham," commented a reporter, "has come solely for the benefit of his health, which fresh air and pills suffice to keep in excellent condition." With clinical detail it was observed that Mr. Beecham was hearty, his hair plentiful, and his teeth sound. He wore check clothes of an unobtrusive pattern, and a rural cut, and his coat, despite the tropical temperature, had a velvet collar. Questioned about his career, Thomas was characteristically brief. All that could be squeezed from him was that "he was born in Oxfordshire, the accent of which county he still retains. He went to work in the fields at eight years. There he had often to treat the ailments of cattle and learnt something about drugs, medicine and herbs. He says that when he felt unwell he compounded some pills of his own use".

On the subject of his wares, and advertising, Thomas waxed slightly more eloquent. His pills, he affirmed, were swallowed principally by the poorer middle classes who did not care to apply for medicine to public institutions. But they were also taken by dukes and lords "who concealed the fact from family doctors". A game of hide-and-seek, apparently, since "medical men took them on the quiet, too".

Asked about his bill boards, Thomas said he did not advertise in places unless he owned the board and site, because bill posters tended to cheat him. Pumped about advertisements on bathing vans and boats he snorted that the local personalities who complained were, in effect, his arch enemies, "Doctors and druggists who weren't troubled by vulgarity, but were jealous of his patent pills". Tackled head-on regarding the incident of the hymn books, Thomas waggishly ceded to have printed the offending verse in a number of hymnals which he sold cheap to a country parson. What, for prudence sake, dare not be admitted in the non-conformist north, made rattling good publicity in the States!

How much of North America Thomas saw, whether he made good his intention of spending thousands of pounds at the Chicago Exhibition, is not known. But young Tom enjoyed every moment. "Since then," he was to write, "I have seen dozens of the same kind of event, but never anything to compare with this." Old Tom, a veteran of hundreds upon hundreds of fairs, and whose zest more than matched his grandson's, was no doubt equally impressed. Of especial interest, after the pavilions, the Horticulture Building, the Wild West Show, and the international villages, was the ingenious piece of apparatus operating on top of the Manufacturers Building. On a clear night this projected information onto the clouds. Perhaps Beecham's had erred in not going in for sky advertising. . . .

Back at home Thomas was ceaselessly occupied. Southport, with its huge, flat distances, elegant shops, and Blackpool beckoning on the horizon, was a stimulating town. Relations trekked out to see him, as once they had journeyed to Granny Morris. Young Tom came quite a lot, grandfather and grandson sharing several temperamental traits. Sometimes there were scenes, the boy's innate dominance conflicting with Thomas's own. Once a teapot was hurled at Tom's head. On another occasion Thomas was heard to shout after hurriedly retreating, but recalcitrant youth; "You wait, my boy, till the shoe pinches!" A prophetic enough warning, as it turned out. Apart from a reference to his trousers, ". . . seen only on octogenarian farmers in distant parts of the land. Voluminous in build, of rough and thick material

and variegated in hue, they perpetuated a design that was probably of vast antiquity. . . . Hitched well up to the chest and
minus that disfiguring line of division in the façade, which only
an inartistic age could tolerate on the grounds of utility", Tom
has referred only obliquely to his grandfather in his autobiog-
raphy. Off the cuff, however, he was to declare that Thomas
"had violent likes and dislikes and prejudices. He was wont to
utter his opinions noisily, and didn't care who heard him. He
was strong-willed, and strong-minded".

In his own youth Thomas had abused time, now it flowed
with health-giving ease. So serenely, in fact, that a notice in the
*Advertiser* on 30th March, 1895, drawing readers' attention to
an announcement in another column seemed to appear almost
by accident. From this, for those who cared to follow through, it
was learnt that Mr. Thomas Beecham, after half a century of
conducting manufacture of the now world famous Beecham's
Pills, had dissolved partnership with Joseph Beecham, J.P. From
henceforth Joseph would carry on the business on his own
account under the name of Thomas Beecham. There were still
some in St. Helens, it was briefly observed, "who remember the
very humble beginnings of the business which has assumed such
colossal proportions".

If there were they withheld comment.

Perhaps townspeople were faintly surprised to be told that
Mr. Thomas Beecham had not retired years ago, anyway. Outwardly nothing had changed. Joseph, with his two skilled
henchmen, Moss and Rowed, ran the pill palace exactly as he
had done since its inception. Thomas put in a nominal stint
every ten or fourteen days. So very, very quietly had an important chapter turned in his life that virtually no-one seemed
aware it belonged to local, as well as personal, history.

PART THREE

# THE OLD GENTLEMAN

# 16

# CUSTODIAN EXTRAORDINARY

THE Old Gentleman, the title now conferred on Thomas by employees at the works, as everyone dubbed the factory, was a literal, rather than a disparaging one. It was also by way of being an anachronism. He wore reading glasses, but otherwise his faculties remained unimpaired. Exercising no power over him, age was simply a technical matter of acquiring years. It never spoiled an insatiable appetite for life. Thomas's was the secret of eternal youth, and partly explains why this section of his biography is by far the shortest. To the last he retained a child's capacity to be continuously curious about the world around him. People were always absorbing, whilst interest in the business he had created stayed daisy fresh.

Though he had retired, Thomas was still the firm's chief adviser. Less officially, and to the embarrassment of his son, he constituted himself its watchdog. Criticism of any kind continued to inflame him, and his correspondence to the press at this period concerning two major policies shows that if anything the years sharpened, rather than blunted, his pen.

For some time Beecham's had been suffering from the malpractices of imitation pills, and of undercutting. They were not the only firm to be plagued by these nuisances. At one point in his career Thomas Holloway had been obliged to take out an injunction against his brother, who sold "Holloway's Pills and Ointment" from an address in the Strand close to his own offices. But as with the advertising, Beecham's, because they were the largest patent medicine manufacturers in the country, sustained the most damage. A brief mention of both is apposite.

Invariably, illicit sales were affected by chemists who, when asked for Beecham's Pills, especially if requested by the pennyworth, were apt to dole out another make—their own, or a brand they preferred to push. In an effort to stop this, travellers were chosen from the pill-making room, so that they could easily detect frauds on their rounds. Sometimes zeal exceeded prudence, and they turned plain clothes policemen. Entering a suspect shop, they would ask for Beecham's Pills, and on being sold another kind, secretly report back to headquarters. A member of the staff would then visit the chemist concerned, and personally caution him. If the warning was ignored, the offender was prosecuted, an injunction being taken out to stop him from further abuses. By the 'nineties these cases had become sufficiently numerous as to constitute a serious waste of time and money.

Occasionally, though not very often, a mistake was genuinely such. A careless or rushed assistant supplied the wrong brand in error. The "culprit" would naturally enough be indignant at finding himself in court for an offence committed in all innocence. Feeling against Beecham's, particularly the sneaky detective methods employed, ran high. And it was heightened by the fact that extremely little money was made from the sales of the pills, anyway.

Matters came to a head publicly in 1891 when a Mr. Buck grumbled to the *Chemist and Druggist* that, ". . . after fifty years trying to do right between man and man" he found himself on the paper's black list as a fraudulent dealer. He would not attempt to defend himself, his conscience did that! But his object in writing was to call the attention of his brother chemists to the extremely expensive manner in which "Beecham conducts these prosecutions". No warning, but to small and poor chemists it spelled ruin, nothing more or less. Continued Mr. Buck, guardedly: "I dare not say all I should like here, but, friends, do not think because you are respectable and honest men you are not to be got into this trap. . . . Let an apprentice through carelessness give out an unlabelled box of pills if Beecham's is asked for, and Mr. Justice Chancery will say you are a fraudulent man." Might he, he begged, ask those who read the above to send him their names and addresses to attach to the protest?

He might, and they came by the dozens.

In the next edition an editorial note observed that the fact that these coorrespondents had signed their letters, was evidence of their good faith. It was to be hoped that the temperate letter from Mr. Thomas Beecham would convince even his critics that he had been as forbearing as could be expected of him, considering his large interests at stake.

Thomas's letter occupied a column and a half, and "temperate" seems to have been an odd description of it.

"Mr. Buck's letter," he fumed, "makes me appear one of the most vindictive of men; and while I did not desire to pose as a paragon of charity and forgiveness, or as a brilliant example of returning good for evil, still I feel I ought to give the facts of the case in such a way that fair-thinking members of the trade with which I have been connected for fifty years may judge better my reasons for calling the law to my assistance."

For some years, he protested, his attention had been called to the fact that he was the victim of frauds. For a considerable while he had warned delinquents by letter, or verbally. They, the wolves in sheep's clothing, had promised to mend their ways. Alas for honour! For, "During 1889 complaints arrived much more frequently; more than one man was found making 'imitation Beecham's' . . . and I found such a system of fraud rampant in some districts that the most forgiving and lenient man would wonder how I allowed these people to go clear after simply apologizing and promising not to offend again". How was his kindness rewarded? "Why, on making inquiries shortly afterwards I found some of these unscrupulous traders had gone behind their word; and when I read in an organ of the drug trade, among local news, a paragraph written by one of its correspondents advising chemists to 'beware', as Beecham's emissaries were on the war-path in that district, (a statement which, by the by was not true) can anyone wonder at my calling in my lawyer to aid me in my tug-of-war against such flagrant dishonesty." The charge made by Mr. Buck, that one chemist per district was singled out as an example Thomas vehemently refuted, since recently five retailers in one town had been proceeded against at a single court sitting. With a trace of his native accent he hoped that there "would be no need for farther protest".

But hope was dashed. The gauntlet had been flung, and for several weeks angry letters from retailers all over the country flooded the offices of the *Chemist and Druggist*. Admitting astonishment at the size of the discussion which had lately figured in its pages, the paper rallied to Thomas's support. The issue could not be more clear cut. When X asked for a pennyworth of Beecham's Pills and sold his own brand instead, he cheated his customers, and Mr. Beecham. Editorial championship evidently appeased Thomas, and he desisted from further diatribes. But no doubt he boiled inwardly at a correspondent's jibe: "What a poor benighted Tory you must be to write about 'honesty' and 'morality' and all such exploded nonsense! We live in the days of progress, 'boycotting', the 'plan of campaign', and that most wonderful of all 'modern developments' the Nonconformist conscience."

Despite the glare of publicity, deliberately or otherwise, fraudulent selling continued to be an irritating time-waster for the next decade or so. But such petty acts paled beside a gigantic deception unearthed in the United States in 1904.

That November, American newspapers regaled the public with the sensational disclosure of the operations of two groups of patent medicine swindlers working in Greater New York. One of these gangs, caught making and distributing Beecham's Pills, actually kept a huge counterfeit plant in the back room of a pharmacy owned by a doctor on Eighth Avenue. Receiving rumours of this, Joseph adopted the Sherlock Holmes method of his own travellers, sailing to America with the express purpose of running the culprits to ground and driving them into prison. He did so by the simple expediency of tricking them into selling their plant to detectives. Some 10,000 dollars worth of counterfeit goods were said to be found on the premises at the time, and nearly 1,500 druggists scattered throughout the country were implicated. So clever was the counterfeiting that in many cases the retailers, though duped by low prices, were not aware that the pills were spurious.

Undercutting, the second bane, had been going on for almost as long as the above malpractices.

Again, a basic grievance on the part of the offenders was the small amount of money made from the sales of the pills. To offset this some shopkeepers were in the habit of displaying them prominently in their windows at cut prices. This, in technical jargon, was known as "a lost leader". Having enticed the customer into the shop it was hoped money would be spent on more lucrative products. Beecham's excuse for refusing retailers a larger profit was that the latter worked on a quick turn-over. However, constantly nagged at by traders, a slight concession was made in January, 1897, when the small buyer was afforded a better chance of competing with the large cutters by the dropping of £5 parcels, on which an adequate discount was allowed. And since buyers at a distance were handicapped by paying carriage, the firm met the expense on all orders accompanied by cash.

At first these measures won Beecham's friends in the trade. Later that year they received information from Southampton that retailers were willing to fall into line and settle prices, if they could obtain the consent of two large firms to do the same, namely Day's Southern Drug Company Ltd., and the International Stores Company. Both acquiesced, and Thomas drew up an agreement by which the 9½d. size box would be retailed for 7½d. the 1s. 1½d. for 10½d. and the 2s. 9d. for 2s. 3d. Hoping to gain the co-operation of other retailers in the country, Thomas sent a copy of this agreement, together with an accompanying letter, to the *Pharmaceutical Journal* and the *Chemist and Druggist*; both papers publishing an account of it on 2nd October.

This time the *Chemist and Druggist* failed to champion Thomas. Beecham's letter, it was contended, would be received with mixed feelings in the trade. Though the prices quoted on the present agreement gave an all-round profit of 10 per cent, and though, with a quick turn-over of, say, once a month, this represented 100 per cent per annum, it still was not a living profit. Roughly, the 10 per cent represented 1d. a box.

More generous was the *Pharmaceutical Journal* which considered it to be entirely within Mr. Beecham's province to fix the price at which he sold his preparations. It was pointed out, though, that the step taken was insufficient to counteract the evil practice of undercutting. The only satisfactory and logical position for Beecham's was to maintain the face prices.

To maintain or not to maintain face prices was, as it happened at this moment a national quandary, the whole question being hotly debated in trade generally.

Supporting the *Journal's* viewpoint was William Glyn-Jones, a letter from whom appeared in the *Chemist and Druggist* the following week. Glyn-Jones (later Sir, and an M.P.), was a powerful figure in the pharmaceutical world. For many years secretary of the Pharmaceutical Society, he ardently advocated anti price-cutting. Two years previously, when a chemist at East India Dock, he had founded a society called the Proprietary Articles Trade Association. Thomas, though in principle upholding P.A.T.A. had refrained from placing his wares on the protected list, since it seemed clear to him that prices could not be fixed by coercion so long as firms existed which refused to be coerced. Ways and means would always be found for buying all the goods such firms wanted, which they would sell at whatever prices they liked, even at a loss. Also, and reasonably, he failed to see why an article in everyday demand should necessarily carry the same profit as one which might be on the shelf for weeks. His pills *were* in daily demand. It was precisely on this issue that the trade was split in two, some shopkeepers siding with Glyn-Jones; others, like William Day of the Southern Drug Company, preferring to sort out their problems by personal methods.

The impression created by Thomas's letter, wrote Glyn-Jones, could not be over-estimated. It was a public utterance on the vexed question of cutting by one of the largest advertisers in the world. But, having said as much, it was in no spirit of antagonism that he had to point out the following facts: "Mr. Beecham offers to send agreements, with the minimum selling prices of his articles ready printed for signature by rival traders in various districts, and offers to go out of his way to coax refractory ones." The outcome of Mr. Beecham's "kindly meant interposition" was that the Southampton chemists who purchased through the wholesale houses agreed not to sell the smallest size below what they paid for them, nor to part with the large size below 6d. per dozen *less* than what they paid for them. In addition they had to pay carriage. To those others who bought direct in £5 lots a profit of something under 10 per cent was secured, the carriage coming out of it. These figures, Glyn-Jones opined, provided the most eloquent argument which could possibly be used in proving the necessity for the P.A.T.A.

To him, but not to Thomas, who gnawed angrily at this bone in both magazines next week.

"I presume I shall be expected by your readers to at least say something in reply to Mr. Glyn-Jones. To commence with, I beg to refer that gentleman to my advertisement which has appeared in some of the trade papers. I do pay carriage on all orders accompanied by cash." Apart from this oversight, Thomas doubted whether very few members of P.A.T.A. would approve of what Glyn-Jones had written. Retaliation could only lead to more extreme cutting, "the very thing his Association aims to stop. Because firms show themselves amenable to reason it should not be construed a sign of weakness on their part. In my letter I expressed a hope that by mutual agreements a better feeling might develop among rivals in the trade, and I must express my surprise at Mr. Glyn-Jones preaching a doctrine of discord at the outset. A good old firm of chemists in Dundee writes today: 'We hope you will not see your way to put your goods on the P.A.T.A. When you advanced the price of your pills last January, a popular grocer here suggested a similar arrangement to the one of the written agreement that the prices 8½d., 10½d. and 2s. 3d. are adhered to by all.' I trust that what is possible at one place may not be found unworkable at others, and that without estranging the millions who buy and take them."

As with the spurious pills contretemps, battle was waged by correspondents in the columns of the *Pharmaceutical Journal*, and the *Chemist and Druggist* for several weeks. Continuing to extol the virtues of P.A.T.A. Glyn-Jones provoked Thomas to another outburst at the end of October.

"I was well aware, when I stepped into the breach to turn selling at cost into a small profit I was laying myself open to a wordy war; still more prepared to see the matter through, and as the vexed question of cutting has continually cropped up over the last twenty years, I should very much like to see the questions as regards patent medicines thoroughly thrashed out. It was my anxiety to see everyone who handled my pills have a profit, which induced me to drop the £5 parcels, and two or three small buyers can join in a £5 parcel as buying at the same prices as the largest buyers. Mr. Glyn-Jones makes a point of 'living profits'. Now, they vary according to the views of the individual. One chemist who rules the prices of a Midland town writes me, 'I am quite satisfied with the profit I make on your pill, my prices are 7½d., 10½d. and 2s. 3d'." Re-iterating this point that 10 per cent profit on an article of a quick turn-over was better than 25 per cent more than one that was seldom asked for, Thomas asserted that every member of the P.A.T.A. and his wife bought in the best market. "Is not the lowest tender accepted when the house wants painting without inquiry as to 'living profits'?" At such time as the correspondence was closed, Thomas added darkly, he intended reprinting it in pamphlet form, a copy of which would be sent to every retailer whose address was given in the directory of the *Chemist and Druggist*. A threat backed up the following summer by a triumphant news snippet to the effect that he had persevered with his efforts to ensure certain profits to retailers of his pills on the lines arranged at Southampton the previous year. Training his sights on London, Thomas was able to publish the names of twenty-one of the "most redoubtable cutters who had agreed not to sell below a fixed rate". William Glyn-Jones had apparently not guessed the precise mettle of the man he was ranged against!

But at least one retailer outwitted Beecham's by an unusually skillful piece of mathematics. "Better than P.A.T.A." (or the firm), he openly confessed to the *Chemist and Druggist* "how it is possible to make a satisfactory profit out of the sale of Beecham's Pills . . . a typical assorted order amounting to £51 11s. 6d. purchased direct, will when sold at Beecham's newly arranged prices, yield a net profit of 10s. I managed to squeeze over 10s. profit out of an outlay of only £1 0s. 7½d. on Beecham's Pills. I don't have to send cash with the order, either, but get a month's credit from a wholesale house". How had he done it? Critics of Beecham's could not wait to learn. Apparently he cultivated the sale of the pills by the pennyworth among a working-class population, "who are compelled to buy even the necessaries of life in as small quantities at a time as possible. It is so easy to explain that pills, like most other things, deteriorate by long keeping". So he gave four Beecham's Pills neatly folded in a bit of white demy for a penny. He took them from a 2s. 9d. box which cost him 2s. 3½d. and contained 166 pills, thus showing a profit of 1s. 2½d. on each box, or 10s. 10½d. on nine.

Nice going! No doubt countless retailers were grateful for the tip, and no doubt but that Beecham emissaries nipped the enterprise swiftly and vengefully in the bud.

Nothing if not protracted, the anti-cutting debate dragged on till 1905, Thomas, content with his outburst, now licking his wounds in silence. But on the point of not joining P.A.T.A. Beecham's were resolute, though in trying to win them over (the biggest prize in their campaign) the society proved equally obdurate.

In October 1898 a meeting of chemists held in the Town Hall, Dewsbury, was attended by Messrs. Glyn-Jones, Rowed, and Glover, the dashing representative. Rowed read out a paper in which Thomas's reasons for refusing to place his pill on a protected list were re-stated. The 1s. 3½d. size box would have been 1s. on it, or it would have been rejected as not worth inclusion. Broadly speaking, the sale of the pills in the British Isles was 100,000 boxes weekly. The audience might consider the check that would have had on business for years to come had they complied with P.A.T.A. wishes. As it was, the audience was suitably stunned to learn of Beecham's flourishing state of affairs!

Four years later Glyn-Jones wrote and asked Thomas to attend another meeting, held this time in Glasgow. An invitation declined on the grounds that "Beecham's Pills being in such demand are sold practically everywhere by chemists, druggists, stores, grocers, co-operative societies, and in fact by anyone holding a medical licence". These various channels were satisfied with a variety of profits. Mutual agreements locally arranged were working out smoothly. These agreements were the only possible protection for Beecham's Pills with their cosmopolitan handlers, many of whom "distinctly state they will not ask for more than 10 per cent. But to make my position quite clear", Thomas concluded, "I have just had an abstract of my home sales made for the last month (the largest October sales ever recorded) and I find that the total orders by customers who are at all likely to be in sympathy with Chemists and associations throughout the British Isles is only about one half, thus showing the large amount of business done in Beecham's Pills by retailers at your meeting". Finally, the steps he had taken to stop undue cutting did not necessitate his forming one of a group.

Nothing could ever have made Thomas, the individualist, join a group, but this was as much a matter of psychology, as of trade diplomacy.

"That gentleman," observed the chairman of the Glasgow meeting, commenting on Thomas's reply, "make a great mistake if he imagines that the other 50 per cent do not want a profit." And on this fractious note P.A.T.A. plus Glyn-Jones, gave up the impossible task of persuading Beecham's to toe their line.

One last word on the subject. The anti-Beecham retailers so discontented with their profits must have been even more indignant at a British Medical Association report on secret remedies made in 1909. This stated that a box of pills as "advertised to be worth a guinea, is sold for 1s. 1½d. and the prime cost of the ingredients of the 56 pills it contains is about half a farthing".

Confided Joseph to an acquaintance: "I would certainly have sold my pills for a penny a box, and still have made a profit of more than a halfpenny on each one. But," he added significantly, "nobody would have bought them at that price. They would have regarded them as too cheap to be of any use. So I sold them at 2s. 9d. and made a fortune."

Just as well for his dependents, and for today's mighty Beecham empire! But it was Thomas, of course, who had originally exploited this human foible in 1860 when he had stepped up the starting price of his boxes from 6d. to 9½d.


17


# THE NEW MAYOR


IN 1897 Thomas added substantially to his property in St. Helens by the purchase of Lord Gerrard's College Street Estate, for which he paid nearly £20,000. Having said this, the chapter belongs to Joseph.

Two years later, in October, the second Boer war broke out. Joseph made a magnificent donation to the South African Fund. November found the Beechams competing for a signed manuscript of Rudyard Kipling's *Absent-Minded Beggar*, the poem being sold for the benefit of the wives and children of the British Reservists.

War was grist to the Beecham's drug mill. So many complaints reached the firm that the pills were unobtainable at the front that Joseph advertised his intention of sending a box gratis to any soldier on active service, providing friends or relatives submitted suitable addresses. For the aesthetic comfort of the troops 1,000 photo-folios, and as many music books, were dispatched to South Africa. Respecting commercial benevolence *The Times* had its grouch. The requirement of the troops during the six days in the field for military manoeuvres "included some articles that were scarcely indispensable to warfare". Among these were "bloater paste, tins of mackerel, toilet soap, and Beecham's Pills".

Fortunately the British Tommy thought otherwise, and Beecham's seized on the spontaneous testimonials which poured in. Describing the bad weather, sharp frosts, and surprise attacks by the Boers, an artilleryman declared he kept pretty well, except for a cold and a nasty rash. However, he had sent specifically to Kimberley for the pills, and thanks to them was serene again. "The doctor gave me some physic which I put behind a hedge and swallowed Beecham's Pills like a Christian." "I forgot to tell you," a soldier in the Coldstream Guards wrote home, "to send me some Beecham Pills, too." (Probably the best affidavit ever acquired was one in 1913, when a man aged 101 averred: "I don't need the doctor or his Physic—a couple of Beecham's a week do for me." They obviously did. Born eight years before Thomas, he was still going strong six after the latter's death!).

By 1899 Joseph was Mayor of St. Helens, having been elected in November by a unanimous decision of the Town Hall Council. If the war swelled his pocket, it also added considerably to his municipal duties. But he managed everything with admirable aplomb, organizing dinners for departing detachments, arranging concerts and relief funds, while at the same time frequently putting in a fourteen-hour day at his desk.

His inaugural (mayoral) concert which he gave on 6th December, 1899, has already passed into music history, since it was the one at which his son, Tom, made his professional début as a conductor. It therefore needs only a quick reference here. For it Joseph hired the Hallé orchestra, also Hans Richter, shortly to be the orchestra's permanent conductor. But several days before the event Richter, somewhat tactlessly, found he had a more pressing engagement. Affronted, faced with the ruin of his evening, and largely from pique, Joseph agreed to young Tom's sug-

gestion that he should conduct instead. When the news was conveyed to Manchester the orchestra threatened to strike. With a
flash of his hidden steel Joseph retaliated by offering to send to
London for other players. The orchestra capitulated. Tom was
then twenty, and the programme, as he later wrote, "went off
without any of the hitches expected in most quarters and hoped
for in some".

From Rossall Tom had gone up to Oxford, but after about
only eighteen months had left, feeling that university life had
little positive to offer him. Given a nominal job at the factory his
duties were of the lightest, and he maddened the works' foreman
by juggling cough and costive pills in the air, and drawling: "Tell
me, dear chap, can you *honestly* tell the difference?" Affecting
bohemianism he grew his hair to outrageous lengths, refusing,
despite parental pleas, to have it cut. He was a musician.
Musicians were different from ordinary people, and that was
that. In his spare time he had formed an orchestral society, whose
players were part amateur, part professional, and with which
he managed to secure several engagements. On learning that a
patient at Rainhill asylum was a fine woodwind player, Tom
had Oldham drive him out in an effort to procure the man's
services. Seeing the long-haired youth leap dramatically from
the carriage the gate-keeper murmured: "Poor chap! I do hate
to see them arrive." Tom's exhibitionism had been cause for local
gossip for a number of years. As a small boy he had been incapable of sitting still in the brougham, bouncing up and down and
generally showing off. To Oldham this was sacrilege, since not
only was it not *done*, but it disgraced him in the eyes of all the
other grooms trotting infinitely better behaved charges around.
The child was reprimanded. No good, Oldham might have been
addressing a stone wall. One day, at the end of his tether, Oldham yanked Tom from the vehicle and administered a sound
thrashing. Subsequently sweetened by the gift of a box of chocolates, these, or the punishment, had the desired effect,
Tom reserving his histrionics for other occasions.

To return to Joseph. The installation concert may have gone
off without any hitches. Perfect though it had been, however,
it had not escaped the criticism to which the Beechams were so
curiously vulnerable. Hitherto bun teas attended by "respectable
folk" had been traditional mayoral receptions. Not a carefully
selected list of guests, not a hall crammed with ferns and flowers,
certainly not a major wearing a gilt-looped black silk hat, crimson gown, sable-edged, and ordered from the Queen's own robe-
maker. Joseph could rise to the occasion when he chose, and

swathed in finery, it was hard to recognize the homely pill-maker the townspeople knew, and who usually did not give a fig for clothes.

But it was the weeding-out of entertainees which had rankled most, and protests had begun to make themselves so warmly felt even before the concert, that at the beginning of December an explanation had appeared in a local newspaper. Some mis-understanding, it appeared, "seemed to exist as to the way in which the lists of those invited to the Mayor's reception and concert had been arrived at". His Worship, however, "wishful to give a really high class musical treat to as many as the Town Hall will seat, was anxious to obtain as far as possible a really musical audience, and to arrive at this the old list of town hall visitors was practically ignored, and a large number of local in-habitants known to have a musical knowledge and who had never been to a Mayoral function were invited". But, it was hurriedly pointed out, the Mayor was to give a children's fancy dress ball in January, while adults (presumably the non-musical rejects) were to be entertained to an At Home in February.

*Really?* A staid tea-party could not have begun to have com-pensated for the humiliation of being excluded from the most glittering function the town had ever known. Evening clothes which had been dragged from wardrobes, shaken free of moth-ball odour, inspected and renovated, had to be returned unworn. It was too bad, especially when it was borne in mind that the Beechams had only emerged from obscurity a decade ago. Whilst ten years before *that*, and never to be allowed to be forgotten so long as a brick remained standing in St. Helens, The Old Gentle-man had been selling his pills from a fish tub in the market-place. Joseph would have done better to temper power with sobriety. Though the press might rave about the splendour of his concert, to the ostracised it had verged on downright vulgarity. It was almost as if the new mayor had been cocking a snook at the past, and past snubbers.

If he was, if hurts, and a protracted social arrival had bitten deep into a complex nature, Joseph was to cock several more. Adding excess to glory he came to out-dazzle even himself. For if anything the Juvenile Fancy Dress Ball was more brilliant than the inaugural concert. Youngsters who attended it remem-bered it all their lives, many of them never knowing a grander function. Again held in the Town Hall, stairs and corridors were carpeted with crimson cloth. The assembly room was restocked with graceful plants and blooms, lit with the softest of electrical glows, whilst a veritable army of stewards waited on the children.

His Worship wore his beautiful gown; His Worship's sister-in-law, Maud Gladstone Beecham, distributed the prizes. Also attending it were five of Joseph's daughters, one of them, Josephine, acting as Lady Mayoress, her mother being indisposed. Painted with musical motifs, and inspiring *The Lady* to praise, were the girls' dresses. Beside such originality the nurses and soldiers fancy costumes of the other children faded to insignificance. After the ball was over the Mayor was presented with a souvenir of the occasion in the shape of a bound volume containing an address, which, judiciously, he had put on display at the factory.

In the coronation year of King George V and Queen Mary, Joseph, mayor again, eclipsed former generosity by bringing an operetta, *The Golden Land of Fairy Tales*, from London to St. Helens, and sending every child above the age of seven to a free showing. In all some 20,000 children attended. Each one was also given a box of chocolates.

Because there had been so little spoiling in his own childhood, Joseph was always particularly kind to poor children. In January 1900, during his first term of mayoralty, forty-five schools in the town were notified that it was his intention to give a day's outing to 800 deserving scholars, eight years of age or over. Teachers were requested to keep a daily record of marks for good attendance, to include three other Beecham articles of faith—punctuality, exemplary conduct, and cleanliness. Eight hundred children duly qualified, and splashed and paddled to their hearts' content one blissful summer day by the sea. The treat, in fact, had such a beneficial effect on school attendance, that Joseph next offered a full-attendance medal to every scholar who did not miss a single day during the autumn term, special provision being made for those prevented by sickness for qualifying. When won the medal entitled the owner to a Christmas entertainment of the Mayor's choosing. Since some 17,000 children were enrolled at elementary schools in the borough it was just as well that the Mayor's purse was large!

"All Councillor Beecham's functions have been as successful as it was in the bounds of human endeavour to make them," the *Prescot Reporter* had purred over the Juvenile Ball. No-one would believe but that the new paths Joseph would strike out for himself in the future "would be other than those flowered with success in the superlative degree".

Nor were they. Joseph's life glowed with attainment and good fortune. His vitality, like Thomas's, was fantastic. A few years later he became chairman of the local electricity committee. He was to be prominently connected, in London, with the National Sporting Club, was attached to the New York Athletic Club, and was so fond of sport that often, on a Saturday afternoon at the end of a crowded week, instead of relaxing at home, he would rush off to watch a football match. Chairman of the Proprietary Articles Section of the London Chamber of Commerce, he participated actively in its work. Before his death he was landlord of the Royal Opera House, London; of the Drury Lane Theatre, the Gaiety and Strand Theatres, besides being proprietor of the Aldwych Theatre, and one more at Warrington. To a knighthood was added a baronetcy. Initially responsible for two spectacular seasons of Russian opera and Ballet at Drury Lane, the Czar of Russia bestowed on him the insignia of Saint Stanislaus, the highest honour conferred upon a civilian in Russia.

But perhaps his greatest achievement was the conquering of provincial puritanism in being re-elected Mayor of St. Helens after a particularly salacious scandal. Nothing more emphasizes his excellence in office than this triumph over small-town conscience. Joseph's detractors might sneer that he had bought his mayoralty by his donation to the Boer War fund. But, and as Sir David Gamble had rightly said when proposing him, his private charities would never be known. And having been elected, by whatever means, he proved himself one of the most efficient, and easily the most ostentatious mayor the town had ever had.

A daughter of Joseph's had deputised for her mother at the concert, and also at the children's ball, because by this date the parents were virtually separated. The sad truth was that they had met only on the plane of music, being incompatible in everything else. Erratic, and subject to depression, Josephine's health had consistently declined as her family increased. Three of her children, Jessie born in 1886, Henry 1888, Elsie 1889, arriving so quickly one after each other like retorts from a pistol, had proved too much. She found it more and more difficult to manage her household, and spent long periods recuperating by the seaside. Despite this, a last child, a girl, was to be born in 1894.

Adding to her debility, Josephine also became afflicted with a form of epilepsy, *le petit mal*, as the French so picturesquely call it. After each attack she was revived with a glass of brandy. Close associates noticed that she came to rely increasingly on alcohol to steady her nerves. During her frequent absences from Ewanville, a Mrs. Davidson, who ran a school at Huyton, acted as impromptu housekeeper. Shatteringly competent, Mrs. Davidson made no bones about the fact that she thought she could have made Joseph a better wife than his own. It was she who had designed the music motifs on the girls' dresses at the children's party. The Davidson set-up, plus inevitable estrangement from her husband, augmented Josephine's unpredictability. Fire to her husband's ice, she was apt to pitch anything at him which came to hand. Once she embarrassed a dinner party by appearing at it in her dressing-gown. On another occasion, entering an Oxford Street store and surprising her husband purchasing a gift for his latest love, Josephine unceremoniously hurled every available muff at him. Economical by upbringing she had been making do with an old fur.

The following incident provides painful reading, but since it has already been described in print, may be briefly alluded to.

In March 1899 Joseph took the drastic step of having his wife incarcerated in a Northampton asylum. Though he had not inherited his father's sadistic streak, he could be relentless to the point of cruelty when he considered circumstances justified strong action. Fond as he had been of his mother he had not flinched from the task of seeking to have her committed when he had deemed it necessary. But now, though supported in his act by doctors' testimonies, it can hardly be said to have been an entirely requisite one. Unbalanced Josephine may have been, but not, according to another mental specialist, to *that* degree. But Joseph was on the threshold of a civic career. He also kept a mistress in London. And so for three years his wife languished in a third-class ward of the asylum. So terrible were her experiences that she never fully recovered from them. During one of her epileptic attacks Josephine fell down near a fire, sustaining a wound on her arm which never healed. Her husband had arranged her committal so secretly that none of her family knew her whereabouts. Tom, and his eldest sister Emily, who, worried by rumours, hurried over from America where she had been studying medicine, instigated a search. The upshot of this was that they tracked down their mother, and the incarceration order became cancelled.

In June 1901 Josephine successfully petitioned in the divorce court for a judicial separation. Alimony, fixed at £2,000 a year was later, and after some wrangling, raised to £4,500. At that time Joseph's income was reckoned to be in the region of £85,000. He was also said to keep £100,000 in his personal current account at the bank, in case "I might need ready cash".

For helping their mother, brother and sister incurred the full acridity of their father's displeasure. Abruptly leaving home,

Tom went to live in London, and did not see Joseph again for nine years. Apart from donations from Josephine, he was completely cut off from financial help. At first he was very hard up. Meeting him one day in London looking extremely down at heel, Oldham suggested Tom went back to Huyton as quickly as possible, and made it up with his father. Tom's reply was pungent. Eventually Joseph foregave him. To Emily, however, he never relented, omitting her altogether from his will.

Approximately two years after leaving Ewanville, Tom married Utica Welles, whose parents were friends of Joseph's. Utica's father, Dr. Charles Stuart Welles, cared for Josephine when she left the asylum. Josephine stayed with the Welles in London, before settling with them at Mursley Hall. In spite of his treatment of her, she had remained fond of her husband, and sobbed on his shoulder to be taken back. This, wisely for both their sakes, Joseph refused to do. Subsequently, and not unnaturally, Josephine grew very sharp with him, refusing offers to be conducted to the opera.

After Utica's parents died, Josephine lived on at Mursley quite alone except for the servants. From time to time her daughter-in-law visited her, and took her for short drives. In old age she became a virtual recluse, retreating more and more into a kind of Miss Havisham existence, frittering her days, and dwelling increasingly, as old people do, on the past. She spoke often of her two avenging children, Emily and Tom, but seldom of the others. She constantly mentioned Lille, from where she maintained her forbears had come. She had made a terrible mistake! Had married Joe the Welshman. Mean old Joe, instead of the Irish boy whom she had really loved. In due course this unknown suitor came to be invested with the incorruptible aura of unconsummated passion. She tended canaries, embroidered, played classical music on an upright piano, leafed through society magazines. Every other day a doctor bandaged her wounded arm. Each night before going to sleep she read in her Bible, afterwards carefully folding it into a silk handkerchief. To the last she retained her trim figure and regal ways, always dressing for dinner even though she dined almost exclusively alone. Her beautiful hair turned white and was drawn back severely from her neat, cold features. Partial senility set in. Her mind would wander, then limpidly return, like a homing bird.

"You could see she was a lady in everything she did," a servant, who had been with her in London, remarked. Adding wonderingly, "Sir Joseph seemed very homely, not at all the person to behave the way he did." Though husband and wife had reached an uneasy truce earlier on, after Josephine moved to Mursley, Joseph never visited her.

Finally, on 3rd November, 1934, and having survived her husband by fifteen years, the Dowager Lady Beecham, as locals called her, died, as she was living, alone. A maid who had been chatting to her in her bedroom went off to make tea. By the time she had brought it upstairs Josephine had stopped breathing.

She was buried at Dent Green Cemetery, St. Helens, close to the little Church of England Chapel. Entombed in the same vault as her husband, the inscription under his own of "Lady Josephine, his beloved wife", chills those who know her story. It was a very quiet funeral, only three family mourners being present, her daughter-in-law, Utica, and Utica's two sons, Adrian and Thomas. Though in England her son Tom did not attend for reasons of his own.

The simple ceremony was in striking contrast to Josephine's own funeral in 1916, and for which more than half the town had turned out. A cortège escorted from Ewanville by the County Mounted Police to the borough boundary, was next accompanied by Borough Mounted Police to the Parish Church, where a service was held. The routes from the church to the cemetery were lined with people, shops closed for the occasion and blinds drawn in tribute. Madame Edna Thornton travelled especially from London to sing "O Rest in the Lord", and mourners included representatives of various theatres, besides one from the Hallé Society, the Lancashire United Railways, and the National Sporting Club. Among the many wreaths was an immense floral tribute from Josephine. With his flair for spectacles Joseph could not have managed arrangements better himself.

Joseph's behaviour to his wife must be partly ascribed to the duality which ran like a black thread through his personality. He could be kind, and harsh. Pathetically vacillating, he yet had an iron will. Unsophisticated, he adored pomp. Unbearably shy, he liked to cut a public figure. At Huyton he worshipped at the Congregational Church, which he keenly supported, but he was buried in conformist ground. Amoral, he was far from being a conventionally match-making Victorian papa. This went deeper than his avowed: "Now I've got t' money I'll see my daughters marry t' blood." The fact was, he could not bear to see them with a man at all. "My father," Elsie has recollected, "told me never to speak to a man. He carried his absurd dictum to the extent of writing to any girl I might be invited to stay with to tell them that I was not to see one."

Having received a free education, Joseph told a reporter of a church magazine that he was, in consequence, "an out and out public man". He "would have them all [elementary schools] freed from denominational control and placed under the control of elected boards". Maybe, but Rossall, where Tom went, had been founded only as far back as 1844 with the express object of providing education for the sons of clergy and laity. Even so, Tom had displayed too much independence, and when it came to his turn his brother, Henry, was tutored by a Staffordshire clergyman in whose house he stayed.

Joseph possessed the Midas touch. All that he handled turned to gold. He wrote well, his letters "could rarely be faulted for grammar or style". In effect he had three successful careers—advertising, pill-making, and, belatedly that of impresario. Proud though he was of these accomplishments, Joseph delighted as much as anything in some window blinds which and with Thomas's gift for handicraft, he had made as a boy. Still in use by a shop in a main street of the town as late as 1927, he never failed to point them out to friends when passing.

"The greatest of his misfortunes," his son Tom has written, "had been the break with myself, which occurred at a time when he needed most the friendship and companionship of a member of his own family."

Another, equally significant, must have been that of having been sandwiched between the extreme extrovertism of the two Thomas's, father and son. He had their brilliance, their tenacity, their panache, but as an introvert he was hopelessly overshadowed.

By 1903 when the separation order had been made, all but Joseph's three youngest children were grown up. Grass widowhood engendered restlessness, he travelled more and more widely. He was to cross the Atlantic fifty-two times, surely a record in those days. London, with its concert halls and cosmopolitanism, had always appealed to him, and a house was purchased in Hampstead. Neighbours, and friends, were Sir W. C. Lever, Bart., and Thomas Barratt. A keen picture buyer, Barratt communicated his enthusiasm to Joseph, finally giving up buying them himself in order to help Joseph build up his own collection. Many blissful hours were passed together in auction rooms. And as might be expected, since Joseph, like his father, did nothing by halves, he came to have one of the finest collections of eighteenth, and early nineteenth century, English paintings in the country. Occasionally members of the public were permitted to view an impressive array of Constables, Cromes, Morlands, Whistlers, Turners, and Mullers, to mention only a few. *The Connoisseur* devoted pages to an account of the collection, reprinted in four parts. This was more than an investment. In common with music, paintings became a passion. Joseph genuinely liked art for art's sake. A favourite habit after the rest of the household had gone to bed, was to fill his pipe, turn out all lights save that illuminating the picture of his choice, and steadily and lengthily absorb every detail.

He had married without Thomas's blessing. When the storm crashed, Thomas did not interfere. Though there was a certain complacency in having his judgement vindicated, Thomas refrained from an "I told you so" attitude. The problem was Joseph's, to be dealt with in Joseph's own way. But there was one, happy compensation, from Thomas's angle. The Beecham suits had made unsavoury reading. Especially lurid was American coverage. The Welles' came from the States, and an ancestor of Dr. Welles, though originating from Warwickshire, England, had risen to be governor of Connecticut. Other important celebrities hovered in the background. "Miss Utica Welles refuses to give up the man she loves though urged by friends to abandon him," shrilled the *Inter Ocean Chicago* at the time of Tom's engagement. "Mr. and Mrs. Beecham have had domestic troubles which have given rise to one of the most sensational divorce scandals of the day. Beecham grew tired of his wife, shut her up in a lunatic asylum, and she could not get out, because there were orders she was to see no-one."

Worried by the scandal, responsible members of the firm had approached Thomas, and asked him if, spending thousands a year on advertising, he could not exert his influence to keep his son's name out of the newspapers.

Thomas's retort was typical, unequivocal. "What, stop old Joe? I wouldn't dream of it! He's the best bit of free advertising I've ever had."

## 18

# LAST DAYS

WHILE Joseph amused himself picking up laurels, Thomas, now in his eighties, had entered the last lap of his life. The straight was gratifyingly peaceful, and behind it lay an astonishing span. A whole revolution, in fact, in time and motion, so that, having recounted it, the beginning seems to have got lost well before the end. For the world of The Old Gentleman's childhood had long since disappeared.

To recapitulate briefly. Thomas had grown up under the reigns of George and William IV; he had become elderly with Queen Victoria; now Edward VII sat on the throne. The dreadful days when a child of eight could work from dawn to dusk seven days a week, when employees might not band together, when executions had taken place publicly, when society was sharply divided into rich and poor, had vanished forever. He had seen the emergence of labour control; the growth of trade unions and the Co-operative Society; of the middle class to which his grandchildren could lay claim, and of elementary education. When Thomas had been a boy people had travelled very little. Then they had gone everywhere by coach, postchaise, private carriage, and on horseback. Those who could not afford these methods had walked. With the macadamizing of roads, coach speed had gradually increased. Public railways were followed by bicycles, electric trams, and the motor car. In 1900 a Zeppelin airship had made a flight of over three miles; seven years later the Aero Club would hold an exhibition in London. Many other inventions and innovations had sprung into being. The telegraph and telephone system, photography, radio, and public libraries, to mention only a few.

Thomas was essentially "with" each new generation. In his own field he had been ahead in improvization. And so he welcomed a changing world, particularly the economies effected by the advent of various machines. Though he had a curious aversion to cars, he enjoyed speed. Broadly speaking, however, he was neither a Georgian nor a Victorian, as, had he been born later, he would have been an Edwardian. A progressive individualist he was always completely himself.

Since he was nearly forty before he found his feet, it is difficult to pinpoint the exact moment when his luck turned. Perhaps it had been in Cropredy, when his herbal experiments had enabled him to renounce shepherding. Or it might have been the day he left Wigan and settled in St. Helens. Undoubtedly the town was "good" for him, in the mystical way that places can be "good" and "bad" for some people. Though slow to advertise, he was fortunate in adopting a winning slogan right from the start. In declaring to a Liverpool reporter that it was perseverance, more than anything else, which had brought him success, he was uncharacteristically modest. He could have added complete dedication to the task in hand, a ribald disregard for adversity, unlimited optimism, sales magnetism, stamina, sincerity, and an ardent belief in his destiny. Apart from his own gifts, his greatest asset, of course, had been Joseph. Left to himself Thomas would have been happy with a prosperous, but contained, concern. The son it was who had turned a golden dream to platinum.

A long life Thomas attributed to semi-abstinence. "I have always believed and practised moderation in both eating and drinking." Finally, he had been fortunate in his inheritance. From the Beechams he had derived balance, industry, and staying power; from the wild Hunt strain, independence. Why the fusion should have achieved such striking results in his case, and not with other members of the Curbridge family, remains a genealogical mystery. Yet the fact is that all the talent, the genius, the artistry, have stemmed from his loins. It is the northern, and not the southern descendants, who have made news; whilst the trio, grandfather, son, and grandson, has been a fantastic one.

Existence at Wychwood was very pleasant. Every ten, or fourteen days, Oldham drove him to the factory in the ancient frock coat he wore for mixing. Locked into the masonic room the all-important business of forming solids and liquids into a pill mass was as fascinating as it had ever been. If Thomas was wanted, a bell would be rung outside, but interruption irked him, and like Nelson clapping the telescope to his blind eye, he invariably turned a deaf ear.

He was still without a personal carriage. For private purposes one was hired from a Mr. Astley who kept stables just across the road. Thomas continued to be fond of walking, but the distances covered were now necessarily shorter, and trains remained an enormous attraction. They moved fast, offered infinite variety, and brought him in touch with life at all levels. Thomas would stride off to the station, buy a ticket at random, then embark on an unpremeditated spree. He might get out at journey's end, or, if the whim took him, continue to an unplanned platform. Adventure was the thing, and each outing was a new experience, a fresh excitement. An added enjoyment, of course, lay in the fact that he could afford to ride in comfort, whereas, when he was young, trains had not only too often been an impossible luxury, but actual ordeals. The hard edge of poverty was never forgotten. *Punch* had perfectly summed up the then and the now of railway travelling in its jingle:

### THIRD CLASS 1837

An open box—a cattle truck,
Exposed to wind, and rain, and muck,
The flap-door falls—a racking plane
Up which you run your truck to gain;
Within, you stand, a herd of swine—
This on a first-class London Line.

### THIRD CLASS 1899

A carpet floor—a cushioned seat—
A toilet service—all complete;
A sixty-mile an hour feed—
A table d'hôte in spite of speed;
A chair in which to sleep or smoke;
All things to ease the travelling yoke;
The panorama rushes by—
A picture pleasing to the eye;
The woods, the streams, the fields, the hills,
Announcing every kind of pills;
You read them all and cannot tell
The pill that's best to keep you well;
So go to sleep before you're flustered,
And dream you're taking "Beecham's Mustard".

Hoardings and enamelled signs bearing his name naturally enhanced the delights, and Thomas cut out, and kept the above.

His appearance which had always been compelling, was, in old age, positively electrifying, often creating a furore when he strode down fashionable Lord Street. A poly-photo shows him wearing a thick overcoat and velvet collar, possibly the same in which he had been interviewed in New York. The eyes stare out burningly above the sunken cheeks, the lips are thin, firm, slightly twisted. A bushy beard, and hair flowing almost to the shoulders adds to the patriarchal effect, whilst the sense of vitality is intense. Mrs. Brooks, Wychwood's present owner, saw him once, when a small girl, and thought "he looked like a Quaker, with his long, flaxen-white hair streaming down onto his broad paper collar".

Locally, Thomas had gained the reputation of being a hermit. "He kept strictly to himself, never entertained, and was most eccentric in behaviour." His garden was well cultivated, shrubs and fruit trees, always top quality, purchased from a nursery in Roe Street. His acquisitive trait had remained strong. When small boys pilfered apples he so far forgot his starving childhood as to have glass embedded into the cement on the high wall. If requiring a gardener Thomas advertised for one by the simple expediency of drawing the figure of a man digging on a piece of cardboard, which he slung on the front gate. While still at St. Helens he must have suffered a spiritual rebuff of some kind, for after transferring to Southport he never again attended church. People, he complained, "Sit there on Sunday with their crooked heads scheming who they will cheat on Monday". But his faith, a straightforward belief in divine providence, was unpunctured, and for any young relatives who might be staying with him Sunday Bible readings were compulsory. Thomas always took the Word literally. Once, when living at Mursley Hall, he had been spotted on a station by a vicar, receiving a new pram intended for his latest indiscretion. Feeling constrained to admonish him the vicar asked if he did not think, in his position, and at his age, it was really disgusting?

Thomas's indignation was equally fierce. "Don't you know," roared he, "that God said unto men, be fruitful, and multiply, and replenish the earth?" He was not being consciously blasphemous. He had been given a male body for a specific reason. Far more serious to him than the venial sin of fornication were faults of character, such as lying or cheating.

Indoors Thomas was never idle. Shut into a room of his house, or in his cellar, he dabbled with his beloved herbs. Scored in his copies of The Art of dispensing and Pharmaceutical Formulas are such widely varying remedies as those for inflamed gums, coughs, linaments, mouth washes, moth solutions, pick-me-up bitters, and mouse and rat poisons. Astrology still fascinated him. Meticulously executed horoscopes of his numerous relations were cast, and shuffled round the family like so many beautifully coloured playing cards. Not all his predictions have proved accurate, but in one case he did foretell a grandson's insanity. Noise breaking in on his reveries he loathed as much as ever, and the cry of "Shut your row" could reverberate with all its old force.

Of his relatives Thomas now saw considerably less than he had done previously, though free pills were readily dispatched for the asking. He almost never ventured south, while Joseph, as has been mentioned, was increasingly absent from Huyton. He seems not to have attended the wedding of his granddaughter, Josephine, in 1905 at Hampstead, and which was reported in the Court Journal. So far had the Beechams progressed! Joseph's second youngest daughter can only recall seeing her paternal grandfather once. "I was a very small brat seated on a lovely cream rug in the dining-room in front of the french windows at Ewanville. Suddenly there appeared behind me an immense figure, or so it seemed to me, in a grey frock coat and a long white beard like Father Christmas. He hardly spoke. He came with the nurse and handed me half-a-crown which staggered me, not having seen one before."

Despite his wealth Thomas practised economies. The duties of a garden boy at Ewanville included removing refuse thrown out by the cook. He had just emptied the day's waste into a bin, and was returning to the kitchen, when Thomas strolled up, inquisitive and prodding. Rooting amongst the rubbish he pulled out some celery trimmings, exclaiming in scandalized tones, "My conscience, what a waste! I must have these stewed for the children."

Occasionally Oxfordshire visited Southport. A grand-daughter of sister Ann, on holiday with an aunt in the town, called unexpectedly at Wychwood. Thomas, who was alone, opened the door. The two women had the impression he was not very well, and had been indulging in a cat-nap on the floor. Nevertheless, he was the soul of hospitality, making tea for them himself, and pressing a sovereign into the girl's hand when the time came for them to leave. Largesse was dispensed, still, providing it was not *asked* for. In one instance grandson Henry was less lucky than this relative. Having heard tales of Thomas's many generosities, he, so the story has it, was seen to enter Wychwood gaily twirling his cane. A little later, and no richer, he crept glumly from the house, his expectancy no doubt having communicated itself all too urgently to his grandfather.

An indirect branch of the family Thomas *did* see a good deal of in his latter years was that of his daughter Maggie, and her family. Hers was the name, it may be remembered, which had been pencilled into the family Bible in 1862, below the inked-in births of Thomas's four legitimate children. Thomas had kept in touch with her ever since, and when Maggie married he had a house built for her in Cheshire. As with the factory, this building had a frieze of heads over the porch never completed, and thought to have been executed by the same sculptor who had so mysteriously disappeared. Maggie had three girls, and two boys, and with this extra posse of grandchildren Thomas was frankly delighted. He visited them regularly, and once took Maggie and a daughter on a rare holiday to a Welsh resort. When the little girl wanted to play the piano, but could not find any music in the hotel, Thomas rushed out, presently returning with a Beecham's music folio jubilantly tucked under his arm.

The girls went to school at Southport, and during the summer months Maggie rented a house there. On these vacations, and on half-days from school, the children trooped over to Wychwood, where they were always confident of a welcome. One of the girls, Lilian, has remembered how Thomas frequently ate his meals standing up, and had no table manners worth mentioning. He was a storybook grandfather, stern but just, easily placated if they behaved themselves. She, her sisters and her brothers all adored him, and were very proud when people pointed him out as a celebrity in the town. "He was the kindest of men. I liked everything about him, except having to kiss him because of his whiskers, and his lips which were permanently damp."

Thomas's rather warped sense of humour is illustrated by the following anecdote. A favourite game of his was to place five shillings on the table in front of these grandchildren, together with five sovereigns. Which would they choose? A truly terrifying problem! For if, displaying greed, they plumped for the gold, they might only be fobbed off with silver. Alternatively, if they said shillings, Thomas was just as likely to dub them stupid, and, as in poor Henry Beecham's case, give them nothing. Much, of course, depended on the mood he was in. Relating this story more than half a century later, Lilian could still feel the hollow pit in her stomach which accompanied each agonizing decision. But once she was paid more spontaneously. They were all, Maggie, Thomas, and the children, returning to the rented house one evening via a horse-drawn tram. Suddenly a gust of wind sent the straw on the floor scudding, and extinguished the little swinging lamp.

Boomed Thomas: "Where was Moses when the light went out?"

Lilian's prompt rejoinder, "In the dark," pleasing him, for he admired quick wits, a coin was instantly pressed into her palm. Thomas, like Joseph, could have a sense of occasion. When the girls went back to school it was always by cab.

Lilian has given several more impressions of him. She and her brothers were often set to do the "rule of three", mathematics remaining imperative. Thomas was extremely partial to champagne, which he drank at any hour of the day, though only in small quantities, and because he liked the sheer luxury of being able to afford to do this. He was often to be seen holding a Bible, which he studied intently. He had an archaic turn of speech, and a capacity for tenderness with this family in direct contrast with his own. At such times as he visited Maggie in Cheshire, Lilian would dash excitedly from the house to greet him. Nor did she ever forget the feel of Thomas's hand cupping her chin, the infinite affection with which he enquired, "Tell me, child, is your mother within?"

Though Thomas, for an unknown reason, had not married Maggie's mother, there seems to have been no lasting bitterness, no scenes of recrimination, no slander. Maggie sometimes called at the factory, but not until one of her daughters became engaged did she reveal the facts of her own birth. Let it be told that the darling grandfather who had sported with her children on the sands, teased and joked with them, packed them off to school tipped and spoiled them in the holidays, was anything other than strictly orthodox. Nor had they ever witnessed the darker, sadistic side of his nature. After much that has had to be written of Beecham unfamily-mindedness, this touching relationship in Thomas's sunset years, makes very happy recording.

A legend in his own life-time, Thomas was the subject of innumerable anecdotes, some amusing, others manifestly preposterous. He always enjoyed showing people round the factory. One day, in Liverpool, he ran into Sir Albert Stephenson, the well-known newspaper man. The two had become firm, if disparate friends, after Thomas's début in advertising. Stephenson was taken back to St. Helens, where, having examined the wonders at the works, he was pressed to stay for lunch. He readily accepted, he and Thomas repairing to the latter's office. Here the desultory talk continued for so long that Stephenson began to wonder if he had mistaken the invitation. But at last Thomas sent for champagne. On its arrival he produced a crumpled paper bag from his pocket, extracted two buns, and lunch commenced.

Another time, when some travelling players were in town Thomas let the entire company inspect the firm. Invited to help themselves to as many pills as they wished, a leading actor complied so enthusiastically that he had to be replaced by an understudy the same evening. And this, apropos of Thomas's shrewd business instinct, which could surmount even his hatred of being swindled. A grocer cheating him, he stormed from the shop vowing he would never set foot in it again. Next day he was back, composedly giving his order. Grumbled the shop-keeper, "I thought I'd seen the last of you." "And I meant you to," Thomas parried, "but you're the only shop where I can get what I want. I'm going to pot some bulbs and I need a fine bit of sand."

Genuine admiration Thomas appreciated, but facetiousness, since he took his wares so seriously, was anathema to him. It was unfortunate that they were an easy target for jokes. Outside Wychwood was a coach stop, and drivers pulling up would crack their whips in the direction of the house, passing pertinent remarks. A Rugby team, training in the town, was taken for a wagonette trip. Turning into Norwood Avenue the driver indicated the Astley residence where Thomas hired coaches, and where a young member of the household was a promising athlete. "On my left," he shouted, "lives the champion runner of the world. And on my right," with a wink and a circular gesture, "lives the man who has made me run faster than I ever have before." Definitely not amused, Thomas, who had been standing by his gate, slammed indoors.

William J. Locke, the novelist, modelled his character of Clem Sypher on Thomas, in his book *Septimus*. There are startling parallels. Sypher, a subsidiary character, was a manufacturer of a cure for bad complexions. He spent millions of pounds a year on advertising, and did not "give a hang for anything in God's universe", save the Cure. Internationally famous, people pointed him out on promenades. ". . . had he chosen to take advantage of his opportunities he might have consorted with very grand people indeed. . . . But he had no social ambitions." Criticism of his Cure brought tears to his eyes. Dreadful, too, was the thought that those "two magic words should cease to blaze on the wooden boxes. . . . The factory had taken its rank with eternal, unchanging things, like the solar system and the Bank of England".

So had Thomas's, in his own mind. He had given Mursley Hall to his grandson as a wedding present, but when Tom made it clear he was more interested in music, tried unsuccessfully to wrest back the estate.

One other allusion is interesting, since it conjures up shades of the Curbridge shepherd said to have passed on his formula to Thomas. It also suggests that it may have been the doctors in Wigan who made things a little too hot for him there, for some reason, whilst boredom with the routine of a chemist's shop caused him to think twice about setting up a fresh one in St. Helens, even had he had the money to do so:

Sypher had owned a chemist's shop, ". . . a little shop in a little town, too small . . . for the great unknown something within him that was craving expansion. The dull making up of prescriptions, the selling of toothpowders and babies feeding bottles—the deadly mechanical routine—he remembered the daily revolt against it all". He liked to talk with an aged man who also "kept a dingy little shop of herbs on the outskirts of

M

the town, also (was) called a pestilential fellow by the medical faculty of the district. . . ." One night the old man, grateful for Sypher's interest in his learning, ". . . gave him, under vows of secrecy", the recipe of a healing emulsion which was to become the basis of Sypher's cure. Interestingly, Sypher had first tried this ointment on a dog, before turning his attention to human beings.

The sands of the hour-glass of life, as he had written so eloquently to Giles in Australia, were now rapidly becoming united to the Angel of Death, and many occasions were last ones.

Curbridge was re-visited. Thomas stayed at the Mitre, in Oxford. Over a meal he quarrelled so violently with the waiter about the tongue served him, tinned and not fresh, that the incident became engraved for all time in the wretched man's memory. Viewed from the outside *only* was the grey stone cottage which evoked so many gay memories. In the evening Thomas stood on Oxford station where, utterly engrossed, he watched the trains pull in and out. They might have been the first he had ever seen, as each mixing session tended to seem a unique experience. His zest for life was incredible.

A letter to the *Pharmaceutical Journal* penned in 1907 was possibly his last to see print, as his final public tirade.

In genuine innocence "C.A.S." had enquired if any reader "Can . . . inform me through your columns, how the colouring of Beecham's Pills is obtained? I mean the outer powder of brown yellow coating, and how it is 'stuck on'? Several makers use this for 'uncoated' pills, but we find it difficult to get".

Kindly, but crassly, a correspondent obliged. The information that the pills in question were coated with the finest light-coloured liquorice powder, and that these should be damped with diluted syrup before it was applied, duly appeared in the next issue.

As might be expected Thomas was convulsed.

To his mind the initials "C.A.S." suggested "Chemist" and "Substitute". The object of the enquiry could be no more than a desire on the part of a trader to imitate Beecham's Pills as closely as possible, "in the hope of deceiving his customers, and my representative, by passing off such imitations as Beecham's if asked for". Since the insertion of the query and answer in the *Journal*, Thomas next rapped editorial knuckles, "may possibly be to my detriment, and probably the cause of a substantial loss to 'C.A.S.' and other unscrupulous traders, as I can always detect even the closest imitations, I must ask you to give prominence to this letter, that it may act as a deterrent to any misguided individual who thinks it wise to run on these crooked lines. I must look upon this, asking and giving advice, as a step directly opposed to my rights, as I feel it advisable to warn your readers that from now I shall cease accepting apologies, or small sums to be applied to charities, from first offenders caught, and in future when I get a clear case against my fraudulent substitutes, I shall place the matter in the hands of my solicitors . . . without any warning of any kind".

A rebuke received in silence by both culprit and editor, though "Gnomon" felt prompted to write in that he felt the offence, if such it was, hardly justified the "torrent of reprisals with which we were favoured last week". What would have been the inference had the enquirer asked to be furbished with a statement as to the *composition* of the pill? No doubt such a mad request would have merited the instant execution of the misguided individual! This time it was Thomas's turn to preserve a dignified quiet. When his name again appeared in the *Journal* it was five weeks later, and by way of an obituary.

Towards the end of February Thomas was driven to the factory where he put in his customary amount of work. To those employees who saw him moving about the departments, majestic as God, no detail escaping his attention, he appeared every bit as hale as usual. Sometime during the day, however, he caught a chill. For about a fortnight he was bedridden. Then, quite suddenly, at five o'clock on Saturday, 6th April, 1907, he collapsed and died of pulmonary congestion. He was eighty-six. Joseph, then in the south of France, who had been warned of his father's indisposition, hurried back to England, reaching Southport several hours before Thomas's death. At the precise moment a picture crashed to the ground, thereby giving rise to yet another family legend, that Beechams frequently die to the sound of tinkling glass.

Obituary notices, which were numerous, stressed Thomas's generosity and perspicacity. In business, commented the *Advertiser*, he had been just and upright, prompt in all his transactions, and respected by employees, "though insisting on the strict observance of punctuality". A page from the romance of industry, was how the *Liverpool Echo* described his career. Perhaps the *Witney Gazette* came closest of all to the secret of Thomas's success in stating that, though no doubt luck had entered into the matter in great measure due to the catch phrase, worth a guinea a box, Thomas had had the perspicacity to see the value of the saying, "which, in 99 cases out of 100, would have fallen on deaf ears". Enumerating on the fortunes made by proprietors of patent medicines, *Tit-Bits* recalled that at his death in 1883 Holloway's personal estate had been returned for probate at £596,555. A discoverer of a consumption cure had left £147,860. F. B. Bengers, of Bengers Food, who died in 1903 left £420,807. G. Taylor Fulford of Dr. William's Pink Pills £1,311,000, and Andrew Pears of Pears Soap, who was to die in 1909 would leave £134,402. Patent medicine paid! The gross value of Thomas's estate was eventually shown at £86,000, but it must be remembered that he had made over the entire business to Joseph in 1895.

By request there were no flowers at the funeral, which took place on Wednesday the 10th, at the Borough Cemetery, Denton's Green, the district which had been so countrified when Thomas had first settled in St. Helens, but which was now extensively urbanised. Spring showers laced a cool afternoon, and Thomas was interred in non-conformist ground in the same vault which contained the remains of his grand-daughter, Laura. Her name was transferred to the back, and it is his simple inscription which catches the public eye from the pathway.

In accordance with Thomas's wishes the ceremony was very quiet, only a few friends, together with members of the family, being present. Notwithstanding this, a number of local residents who had succeeded in discovering the time the funeral would take place gate-crashed proceedings.

Pall bearers were loyal members of the staff; J. C. Allen, the works engineer with the splendid tenor voice; W. Ackery, foreman joiner; E. Lowe, another foreman; T. Metcalfe, warehouseman; J. Parr, foreman of all the works; and George Oldham a foreman packer, and Tom Oldham's brother.

In his address the Rev. G. E. Cheeseman, Minister of Huyton Congregational Church, who conducted the service, said that Thomas was as remarkable as the monument reared in his name. There were no lurking deceits in the man, or cunning complexities in his nature. As open as daylight, there, was, indeed, a refreshing candour amounting almost to brusqueness. He had his faults, but what man had not? And though not born in St. Helens, the town had in him a citizen of true allegiance, and "they buried him amidst the tokens of respect of his fellow-men, who admired his strong individuality and sturdy honesty".

The same day the *Advertiser* carried a front page advertisement for the pill. The slogan, which was not the famous one, ran, "Life is not to live but to be Well". A fitting enough epitaph, though for sheer aptness a phrase of Goethe's can hardly be bettered. *"Es bildet ein Talent sich in der Stille, Doch ein Character in dem Strom Der Welt"*—Talent develops itself in solitude, character in the stream of life.

Nothing could be truer of Thomas. His gifts had matured in shepherd solitariness, while the market-place had moulded and stamped his nature—the "ever-shifting sea" of humanity which had exercised such peculiar attraction for him.

# INDEX

# INDEX